Read abo

- world-class attractions such as Uluru, the Bungle Bungles, the Great Ocean Road, the Whitsunday Islands, Kings Canyon and Kakadu

- the lesser-known but still highly rated places such as Plane Henge, Parachilna Gorge, Mallacoota, Shark Bay and The Pinnacles

- the unique wildlife, such as kangaroo, wallaby, emu, echidna, dingo, wild camels, the fabulous colourful birdlife and feeding dolphins

- the remote Outback and the challenging desert tracks

- a short spell of hospitality, courtesy of the Australian health service

- the small towns and communities of Australia and their friendly people

- celebrating Christmas in November on a remote campsite with an Australian family

- four murders and an unexpected new baby!

What people are saying about Vic Quayle

"What an adventure! Vic and Pam packed so much into a few months and had such a wonderful time."

"It just shows what's possible if you set your heart on undertaking an adventurous trip. Amazing places to see, people to meet, and terrific experiences. Vic captures them all in his book."

"Poor old Matilda. She had a hard time but came through in one piece, and so did Vic and his wife. I wish I had been with them."

"Vic captures the spirit of the real Australia away from the populated areas of the East Coast, places where men and women must be resilient, hard-working and hard-playing. A great read."

An amazing adventure by motorhome

WALTZING MATILDA AROUND AUSTRALIA

Adventure before Dementia!

VIC QUAYLE

Published by
Filament Publishing Ltd
16 Croydon Road, Waddon, Croydon,
Surrey, CRO 4PA, United Kingdom
Telephone +44 (0)20 8688 2598
Fax +44 (0)20 7183 7186
info@filamentpublishing.com
www.filamentpublishing.com

ISBN 978-1-910819-19-7

Printed by IngramSpark

Maps by Business Maps Ltd

Contents

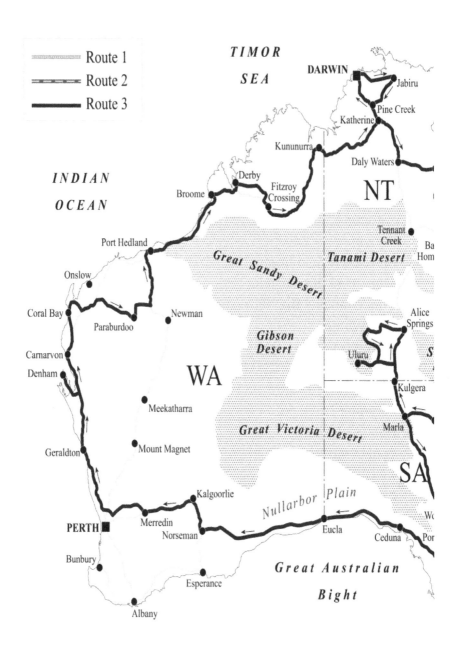

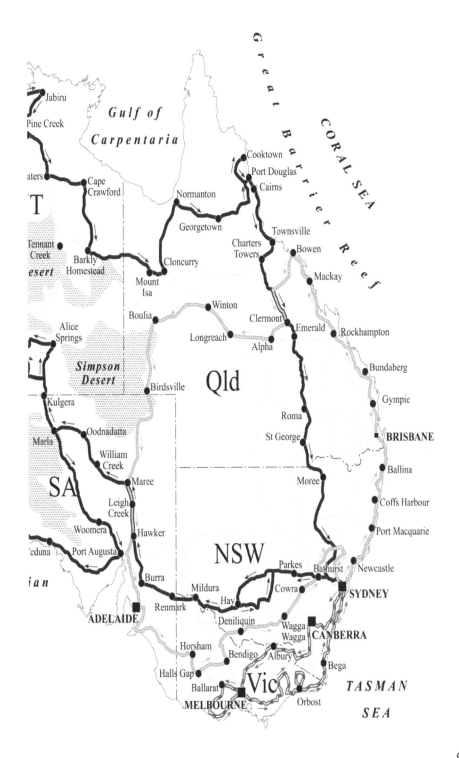

"Do just once what others say you can't do,
and you will never pay attention
to their limitations again."

Captain James Cook

Prologue

As we headed south on the Stuart Highway, we stopped briefly for fuel at Cadney Roadhouse. Now back in South Australia after our sojourn in the Northern Territories, we began looking for a free stop for the night beside the road.

We pulled off the road at Matheson Bore, where we had heard there was a suitable stop, and found two rigs already parked up. Stopping nearby, we wandered over to introduce ourselves and to check they didn't mind us parking nearby. Soon the cold beers were opened and we had yet more new Australian friends.

Debbie, Laurie, Bob and Carol were very welcoming and were friends from Melbourne travelling together with their own rigs, one couple with a caravan, the other with a camping trailer.

Bob and Carol had prepared a huge chicken curry that was already cooking on an open fire in true bush style and we were invited to join them as they were celebrating Debbie's birthday. So we added some cheese and biscuits, some beers and a bottle of wine and sat around yarning (chatting) for several hours under the stars, the only disturbance being the road trains passing on the main road, all lit up like cruise ships on the ocean.

Late in the evening, a birthday cake was produced together with some Baileys, and we all sang Happy Birthday.

Another great evening with people we had never met before but who briefly welcomed us into their lives – great Australian hospitality we sampled time and time again in our travels in Matilda.

A few days later and we parked up on the beach at Streaky Bay, a lovely, small, country town where we could easily have stopped for many days. The campsite was full so we had lunch on the beach and headed on to Fowlers Bay, a quiet, fishing community where the fish meals were five star and the friendly campsite owners put on a BBQ and we ate and drank with about 20 other Grey Nomads until late.

"Don't worry about the world
coming to an end today.
It is already tomorrow in Australia."

Charles M. Schulz
(Cartoonist)

Part 1

*** When in Australia
do what the Grey Nomads do
* Heading into Sydney
* Meeting Matilda**

When in Australia do what the Grey Nomads do

Australia is a country that is perfect for those who love motorhoming, caravanning and camping.

It has great weather with wonderful, blue skies and warm temperatures. If it gets too hot, one can travel south to cooler climes, and likewise, if it becomes too cool, one can venture north and find warmer regions. This is something thousands of Australian Grey Nomads do on retirement; they take to the roads in their motorhome or caravan and often spend the rest of their lives wandering the highways and byways, enjoying the freedom of a carefree lifestyle.

The landscape of Australia is another draw. Whilst much of it is desert with a rugged charm, there are tropical forests, wild mountain ranges, wonderful vistas and beaches, all usually easily accessed by a recreational vehicle (RV). There are dramatic natural features such as Uluru, the Blue Mountains, the Great Ocean Road, and great national parks such as Kakadu, Litchfield Park, Purnululu and Kings Canyon.

There's more: the vibrant, cosmopolitan cities have their own attractions, the most notable being Sydney with its Harbour Bridge and Opera House, but any keen sportsman will know of the MCG and the WACA for cricket, and there is Albert Park and Mount Panorama for petrolheads. There is plenty for foodies too, with renowned vineyards in the Hunter Valley, the Barossa Valley and Margaret River, as well as wonderful fish, meat, vegetables and fruit.

Australia has unique wildlife, notably the kangaroos and wallabies, but also cuddly koalas, not so cuddly dingoes, and domesticated animals gone wild, such as camel, horses and donkeys.

I could go on, but the country has something for everyone. In an RV, it is easy to tour around as there are plentiful campsites with great facilities, and for the more adventurous, free camping almost anywhere outside the main urban areas.

What's more one can get a tourist visa for up to a year. This allows plenty of time to see much of what Australia has to offer as well as complete the Big Lap; what Australians call the trip right round the edge of their country, about 12,800 km (8,000 miles) on Route 1, the main road.

For us, Australia had other possibilities – the Outback, with its remote, small, rural communities, the friendly people, and the more modest attractions, natural and man-made, that appealed.

Although we were keen to visit many of the well-known locations, we also wanted to travel off the beaten track, away from the main tourist areas and experience life in rural Australia, especially the Outback.

We have been lucky to venture into rural areas in many parts of the world. A car rally in South America took us into the remoter areas of both the Atacama Desert in Chile, and into Patagonia in Argentina, as well as the High Andes mountain range. The Christmas 2014 edition of BBC's *Top Gear* covered just a small part of where we went and there was little tarmac when we were there.

Namibia, the least populated country in Africa and which is almost totally desert, has also been on our travel itinerary, the Namib Desert with its huge dune formations being a particular attraction together with the iconic African wildlife that is a particular draw.

So it was inevitable that eventually we would want to pay a visit to Australia. Some impetus was put into an outline plan to go there when our eldest daughter announced that she and her husband were going to emigrate to Sydney with the long-term aim of becoming permanent residents. Soon after they went, an opportunity arose for us to join them for a three-week visit to their new home in the Sydney suburbs. Whilst we hit the usual tourist spots – climbing the Harbour Bridge, taking a tour of the Opera House and visiting Taronga Zoo, we also hired a car and ventured out through the famous Blue Mountains and on to the edge of the Outback in Bourke.

Here was a new world far removed from the cosmopolitan life of a city like Sydney. We found small country towns with friendly, hard-working people and an approach to life hardened by a tough environment, fierce weather and the usual financial ups and downs found in any rural community. But it was real; these people had no airs and graces; they were down-to-earth and lived their difficult lives to the full. It was great.

We also did some interesting driving in our little hire car along gravel roads beside the Darling River to Louth, Tilpa and Wilcannia before heading to White Cliffs to stay in an underground hotel.

I was convinced; we had to come back and see more and experience what many Australians do on retirement: they become Grey Nomads.

At the end of our stay in Sydney, I visited an outdoor and camping exhibition at Randwick Racecourse and spent all day doing research into what was to become an extended visit to the country. I came away with maps, brochures for motorhomes and outdoor equipment, information about national parks, and much more.

I also read a great book about Australia by that well-known author, Bill Bryson. In *Down Under*, he makes whimsical observations about Australia, its peoples and their way of life. In particular, I was drawn to these comments:

Australia is a country that exists on a vast scale. It is the world's sixth largest country and its largest island. It is the only island that is also a continent and the only continent that is also a country.

It is the driest, flattest, hottest, most desiccated, infertile and climatically aggressive of all the inhabited continents and still Australia teems with life – a large proportion of it quite deadly. In fact, Australia has more things that can kill you in a very nasty way than anywhere else.

This is a country where even the fluffiest of caterpillars can lay you out with a toxic nip, where seashells will not just sting you but actually sometimes go for you. If you are not stung or pronged to death in some unexpected manner, you may be fatally chomped by sharks or crocodiles, or carried helplessly out to sea by irresistible currents, or left to stagger to an unhappy end in the basking outback.

Australia isn't as bad as that, but it struck me as a country worthy of further investigation.

A few years passed, and eventually Pam and I decided that as a post-retirement trip we would take a year to visit New Zealand (six weeks in a hired motorhome), then head to Sydney and buy a motorhome and head off to see as much of Australia as we could, as well as our daughter and son-in-law, of course.

Heading into Sydney

And so it came to pass that we landed at Kingsford Smith International Airport, which happens to be alongside Botany Bay where Captain Cook made his first landing, and started our own great adventure in the wonderful country and continent that is Australia.

At the time, our daughter was living in Manly, a beautiful seaside suburb of Sydney. Manly faces the Tasman Sea with a wide arc of golden sands where surfing is very popular. Manly is sited on an isthmus and whilst to the east is the open sea, the opposite side of the town abuts Sydney Harbour with a ferry terminal and a regular service to Sydney CBD (Central Business District) making it a popular commuter base.

Jenny was renting a former fisherman's cottage on the waterfront of Manly Harbour, only a few minutes' walk from the centre of town and the ferry. It had great views across the water to other residential areas, and also down to the main waterways of Sydney Harbour, although the bridge was out of sight, blocked by Middle Head, part of Sydney Harbour National Park.

After a couple of days catching up with family, getting grounded and into the Australian way of life, it was time to apply ourselves to the job in hand – buying a suitable vehicle for our travels.

From the UK, I had been monitoring the websites of motorhome dealers in and around Sydney for many months so as to keep a close eye on what was available and might be suitable for our needs. What we bought would influence the type of trip we could undertake, and this would depend on what the dealers had in stock. Had Matilda, our eventual purchase, not been on the market, we could well have bought a conventional two-wheel drive motorhome. That would have limited our Outback adventures a little, but not much.

Only the wildest parts of Australia need a FWD vehicle, and whilst we didn't head to these very remote and out of the way areas, Matilda gave us more confidence to travel the many gravel roads and venture down some of the iconic desert tracks. With my driving background, I was keen to do some off-road driving and had gathered together a lot of information on the main desert tracks in the hope that we would do at least a couple of them.

We also needed a fully equipped vehicle as it would be our home for nearly a year. I also recognised that we would have to decide pretty quickly what to get as we didn't want to sit around in Sydney waiting for the perfect vehicle to turn up. A compromise would probably be needed before we handed over any money.

I had joined the Campervan and Motorhome Club of Australia (CMCA) as an overseas member and was getting their monthly magazine which has a Members' Market section with 50-60 motorhomes for sale in every issue. Here was a good selection of possibilities, and the magazine, together with the CMCA website, had given me a good insight into Australian RV practice.

Just as in the UK and Europe the variety of motorhomes available, new or second-hand, is enormous. Because of the space available in Australia motorhomes are generally a little bigger than at home and they range from huge fabulously specced coaches, down through the more usual coach built and A class models, to smaller van conversions and backpacker units.

Caravans are also very popular and these too varied enormously, and given the weather that Australians are lucky enough to enjoy, camping trailers are a common investment as well.

At home we had not been fans of caravans, having owned a conventional motorhome for several years before heading to Australia. Within the RV fraternity, one is either a chugger or tugger, and there are advantages to both approaches. Caravanners (tuggers) have the advantage of a vehicle to use once settled at a camping spot, while motorhomers (chuggers) have the luxury of being wholly self-contained, quite literally travelling like a snail with your home on your back.

We had sold our motorhome as well as two cars before we left for our trip; the finance raised being the basis for funding whatever we bought in Australia.

The Sydney RV Centre was the major dealer in the area and at the time had two sites, one at Penrith in the far western suburbs of the city, the other at Narrabeen, for us a short drive up through the northern suburbs from Manly, so I paid a visit and took a look at what they had on offer.

Meeting Matilda

They had a range of caravans and motorhomes and one immediately caught my eye – a six-wheeled Toyota Hilux with a fibreglass Matilda accommodation module on the back.

Matilda, as she immediately became known, seemed ideal for us. With FWD, she was suitable for some off-road driving, she had fully self-contained accommodation, and was clearly designed for driving into remote areas in safety.

On the downside, she had a V6 petrol engine, being a Toyota as solid as a rock, but not good as a diesel. In remote areas, petrol can be a bit scarce as most 4x4s have diesel engines. Oddly, to make up for the petrol engine, Matilda had an LPG conversion, which extended her range and I knew was fairly readily available in the Outback.

More importantly, she was ten years old and looked a bit unused. It turned out that Matilda had been in storage for a long time. This accounted for the low mileage, which was only 77,000 km (48,000 miles), low by Australian standards.

Older vehicles that have been in storage for a long time can be a problem. Mechanical things like to be used so that lubricants are dispersed and interact with the various surfaces; if lying idle, they can get jammed up and sticky. In addition, tyres tend to suffer, and those on Matilda were a mixed bunch, and anyway they were perished. I was prepared to risk these issues on the basis that Matilda would come with a three-month warranty and, initially at least, we would be sticking to busy, populated areas so we could get garage assistance if needed. As it turned out, we were glad to have the warranty as during the first few weeks, we did have some problems with Matilda, but overall she turned out to be the ideal vehicle for us and we grew very fond of her.

I was born in the Isle of Man. I'm a Manxman, and happened to be wearing an Isle of Man TT baseball cap when I visited the Sydney RV Centre. It turned out that the salesman, Martin, had spent time on the Isle of Man in his student days, studying at a research facility just below where my brother lives in Port Erin. An easy rapport was quickly established.

Matilda seemed to be a good option for us, so a test drive was arranged for the next day, and with a full service and a complete set of new tyres included in the price, a deal was done.

In addition, Martin, and his boss, Michael, also from England, helped us minimise additional registration costs that one has to pay on buying a vehicle. Matilda had been registered in Queensland, so had their registration plates. To re-register the vehicle in our name in New South Wales, we could use our daughter's address but there would be complications. We would have to organise the equivalent of an MOT for both the vehicle and also for the LPG system, which was pressurised. This second test would be an 'as new' test and would be expensive. Sydney RV Centre suggested an alternative.

They knew someone in Queensland who could act as our 'agent' and become our base address and if we travelled there within a reasonable time, we could get the vehicle re-registered there. The GST (Goods and Services Tax, similar to VAT) would be less, and the LPG test would be routine, rather than the complete 'as new' test that would be required in New South Wales. This seemed sensible, and would save thousands of Australian dollars, so we agreed. Sadly, there would be a tragic end to the arrangement, one we could never have foreseen.

Matilda parked overlooking the Great Australian Bight

So we became owners of a Toyota Hilux Matilda Crystal III motorhome. Anyone who has ever watched the UK version of *Top Gear* will know about their red Hilux, which was once mounted on the rear wall of the studio. Clarkson, Hammond and May tested it to near destruction by chucking it into the River Severn, driving it up and down flights of steps, and putting it atop a ten-storey block of flats being demolished. Once retrieved from the rubble, it still started up! Toyota Hiluxes are very strong, reliable, and can cope with rugged conditions, which is probably why terrorist groups are seen on television with their artillery mounted on the back of their Hiluxes.

So Matilda was strong. She also came with a raised suspension, a snorkel that provides air to the engine when driving through deep water, a bull bar – an essential piece of equipment in rural Australia - twin driving lights, and a CB radio.

Being an older model, four-wheel drive was engaged by having to stop the vehicle, get out and twist a lever on the front hubs - a chore, but one I never found to be an inconvenience. Matilda had six wheels, the extra pair of rear wheels being a lazy axle, really only there to help carry the weight of the accommodation.

The fibreglass accommodation module was fully equipped. It had a toilet/shower cubicle with a familiar Thetford cassette for toilet waste, a four-ringed gas cooker, gas oven/grill, sink and large drainer, microwave, colour TV, fridge/freezer, air conditioner (in addition to that in the cab), wardrobe, and three wide and deep drawers under a huge worktop, something that is very unusual in a motorhome.

There was sleeping for two over the cab, and the rear lounge/dining area with its table converted to form another double bed, if needed.

Outside there was a 13 amp hook-up, tow bar (something we never used), external H&C shower, and a large water tank for freshwater. Solar panels were mounted on the roof as well as a roll out Fiamma awning.

A couple of drawbacks were apparent. With six wheels, the risk of a puncture was that bit higher and there was only one spare wheel and tyre: with plans to travel into remote areas, I would have liked another spare but there was simply nowhere to mount it. We would also have liked to have space to carry extra fuel in jerry cans, but again, there was simply nowhere to mount them easily.

The other problem was the lack of what I call 'dirty' storage; in Matilda's case a rear boot in which space was rather limited for a spare LPG cylinder, tools, groundsheet, table, chairs, hoses for fresh and waste water, and such like. We would, and did, live with the compromises that Matilda offered us.

Narrabeen is a lovely suburb and the dealership was near a pleasant lagoon, and close to Sydney's major campsite. As part of the deal, the dealer included a couple of nights' stay and a visit from their service manager. He spent a couple of hours showing us all the intricacies of Matilda's inner workings, something every motorhome owner will know can be a bit complicated, but which we were fairly familiar with anyway.

There followed a busy couple of days as we readied ourselves for departure. Coming into Australia as tourists, we had no tools or other accoutrements that we would need for our trip, so we hit the local shopping mall at Warringah and stocked up with sheets, duvets, towels, saucepans, plates, cutlery and other kitchen essentials. I found a couple of car accessory shops to buy a tool kit, better jack, puncture repair kit, air compressor, groundsheet, table and chairs, and a few other bits and pieces that one inevitably needs. Food was last on the list – tinned and fresh – and at last we were almost ready to go!

On neighbouring pitches at the campsite were two large Winnebago motorhomes and pretty soon we were socialising with the occupants. One was occupied by a couple in their late thirties who were permanently on the road towing a small 4x4 travelling the country picking up work from time to time, and very happy with their lifestyle. The other was a similar motorhome occupied by the mother of one of the couple, and she was also content motoring round the country on her own, living entirely independently and meeting up with her family from time to time.

I had heard about a directory of free and very cheap campsites, *Camps 6*, and she had a copy which she considered to be her bible. It had mapping and full details of more than 3,500 sites where one could pull up for the night, or longer, often at no charge, others for a small charge. We would need one in addition to club membership of the various campsite providers so we could take advantage of their discounts.

"Australia is about as far away as you can get.
I like that."

Andre Benjamin
(American musician)

Part 2

* Heading off in Matilda

* Byron Bay

* Bureaucracy

* Loggerhead turtle egg laying

* Matilda fails us

* Whitsunday Islands

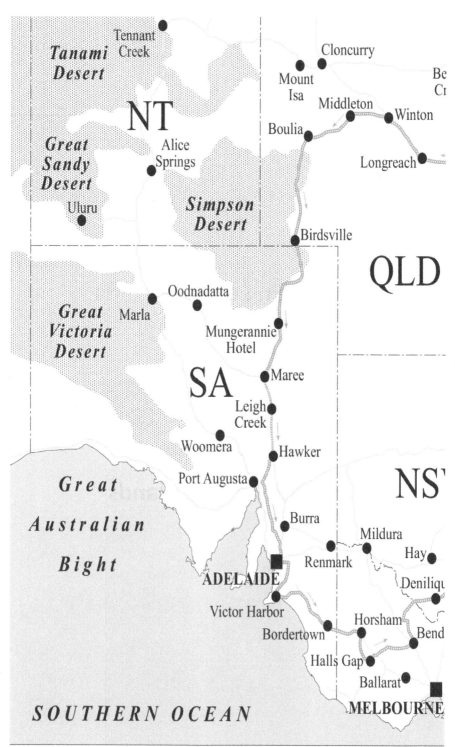

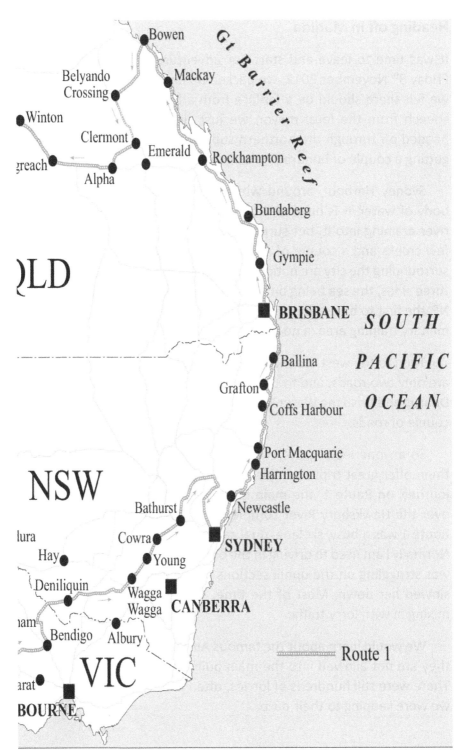

Heading off in Matilda

It was time to leave and start our adventure so the next morning, Friday 9th November 2012, we packed up and got ready to go. Whilst we felt there should be a fanfare from a brass band and a send-off speech from the local mayor, we just slipped out of the site and headed off through the northern suburbs of Sydney with the aim of getting a couple of hundred miles in by evening.

Sydney Harbour, around which the city is built, is an amazing body of water. It is huge and one might expect there to be a major river draining into it, but surprisingly that isn't the case. There are a few creeks and a couple of minor rivers, but that's it. What there is surrounding the city are national parks (NP) almost all the way around three sides, the sea being on the remaining side. To the south is Royal NP, the first to be established in Australia, adjacent to which is a large military training area, a no-go area for the public.

Then to the west are the Blue Mountains NP through which there are only two roads, and to the north are a string of parks, the Yengo, Dharug and Brisbane Water NPs, and through which there are another couple of roads.

So anyone leaving the city has a limited choice of route. All of them offer great trips through wild forest areas, and the start of our journey, on Route 1, the main road north, offered tantalising views over the Hawksbury River complex and massive eucalyptus forests. Route 1 was a busy, six-lane, dual carriageway and at times very hilly. Normally I am used to driving in the outer lanes, but we found Matilda was struggling on the uphill sections as the weight of the bodywork slowed her down. Most of the time, we were in the nearside lane mixing in with lorry traffic.

We would learn about the famous Australian road trains later, but they are not allowed into the main built-up areas on the east coast. There were still hundreds of lorries, often with two large trailers, and we were keeping to their pace.

Pam was on the maps, but the way ahead was pretty obvious; we just wanted to keep on the main road for the day and get away from Sydney. At Newcastle, the road swung left over a large bridge so as to cross the Hunter River, but somehow we missed the road signs and ended up heading towards the city. It was only a minor diversion but it reminded us of the need to keep our wits about us, so we had to do a twirl and get back onto the main route again.

The weather was overcast, but fairly warm, and as it was only a few miles off the main road, our target for the day was a modest seaside resort near Taree called Harrington. We had no trouble finding it, checking into the campsite and setting up camp on a pitch backing onto the road into town.

We were relieved to arrive and complete our first day in Matilda. I was learning how she handled, how all her kit worked, and had started making a few notes of things we needed to investigate further or try out.

Whilst we enjoy our motorhoming, we always find it a rather sedate occupation and make a point of getting a good walk or swim in each day, so we locked up Matilda and took a path through some woods adjacent to the camp and eventually found ourselves on the main beach. The sun was setting behind us, but the wind was brisk and blew the cobwebs away. Later, we had a meal in the motorhome and headed to bed promptly and slept soundly.

Day two dawned with more overcast cloud, and as we headed off from the campsite to the main road, we were soon motoring in rain. We had no grand plan for where we would head other than to keep going up the coast, and it wasn't long before we stopped in the town of Kempsey. Pam went into the local Coles supermarket, the equivalent of Tesco or Sainsbury's, while I checked over Matilda. We were parked in a car park alongside the Macleay River and the Jacaranda trees were in full bloom, their blossom littering the street with their blue petals. Being red/green colour blind, I don't often enjoy the sight of plants as I don't see the full colours they display, but I have no problem with blue and the picture before me was as beautiful as I had ever seen, the petals covering the car park and footpaths all around.

In the afternoon, we decided our destination should be Yamba, also down by the coast, and just as we left the main road, the heavens opened and we had a full-on tropical rainstorm with the rain bouncing off the road and forming an almost impenetrable spray that was very difficult to see through. We pulled over and stopped for a while, and once the rain eased, we headed along a series of side roads to the campsite. We checked in, but the rain started again and once I had driven round to our pitch, we didn't leave the van at all until the morning; it was so bad.

The site was awash with rainwater the next day and we splish-splashed out of the site and headed into the small town of Yamba, found a camp shop and bought some more camping bits and pieces we hadn't picked up in Sydney.

On the way out of town, we came across numerous amazing hot rods, cars from the 1930s, '40s, and '50s, converted into modern vehicles with tuned up, often V8 engines, wide tyres, all in great condition and clearly cherished by their owners. They were having a meet at a local holiday camp for the annual Yamba Hot Rod meeting.

Byron Bay

Our target today was Byron Bay, the most easterly point on the Australian mainland and a popular resort with a great sandy beach, and at the point itself a lighthouse. As we were driving, we noticed a ticking noise coming from the nearside of Matilda and even after a couple of stops we couldn't trace it. Then heading into Byron Bay, a short length of rubber from the windscreen surround came adrift and was flapping in front of us. The problem – it was gradually pulling away along the windscreen edge, so some tape fixed it temporarily and we headed on into town.

Byron Bay is a popular backpacker destination and the town had a lively, youthful atmosphere. There were lots of restaurants, boutiques, bars and surfers and we had already decided we would stay for a few days to catch our breath and work out where we would head to next.

We knew when we started planning our adventure that we would need to be flexible and be prepared to make changes and adapt our plans as we travelled along. Initially we had aimed to get to Sydney, buy the vehicle and spend our time until Christmas travelling the south-east of Australia, maybe Tasmania as well, before heading back to our family for the holidays. Then we would drive off for about eight months broadly circling the continent before returning to Sydney and flying back to the UK. The plan was for Jenny and Daz (our daughter and son-in-law) to fly out and join us somewhere en route, perhaps in Alice Springs or Darwin.

However, a few weeks before we left the UK, Jenny had announced she was pregnant, with the baby due in mid February. This was great news, but meant we needed to rethink our plans as clearly we would want to be in Sydney for the birth, and maybe for a while longer if Jenny wanted our help.

So this led to us completely rethinking our plans and for the first few weeks I hoped we might make it as far north as Cooktown, and then return to Sydney via inland routes in time to celebrate Christmas and New Year with our family. Cooktown was on my wish list of places to visit as I am a great fan of Captain Cook. His ship, *HMS Endeavour*, nearly sank on the nearby coral reefs and he just managed to make it into the river mouth for repair, so the town is named after him.

In the Visitor Information Centre in Byron Bay, I learned that Captain Cook had been there too. He had anchored there in 1770 and named it after another great sailor of the time, James Byron. The Visitor Information Centre, like the many others we sampled in our travels, was a source of much useful information and we nearly always made them our first port of call in any town.

We checked into a campsite that was very full, and we were squeezed onto a small pitch with limited space. We set up camp and made ourselves comfortable and I soon heard an almighty noise from a very throaty engine, and the lorry it powered pulled up onto the next pitch.

Imagine a 1940s' Commer Flatbed lorry, the sort of truck that would do 40 mph at a push and normally struggle to get up any hill. On this example, the cab showed many years of wear and tear, had some gentle rusting and had a lovely patina of ageing. However, this lorry had a strengthened chassis, a new hardwood base for the flatbed, and underneath, mounted behind the cab, a highly tuned Chevrolet V8 engine running on nitromethane. This was one very fast, fiery truck, neatly packaged behind its camouflaged cab; it was one amazing vehicle and had a 0-60 mph time of about five seconds. It had been at the hot rod festival at Yamba and the owner was having a few days holiday before driving home. He was sharing the trip with his daughter in another paradox; a 1950's caravan completely rebuilt and re-equipped with all the usual modern accoutrements one expects in a modern caravan, but in one that looked 60 years old.

We lazed around for a couple of days in Byron, and the weather improved as we walked along the beach and up to the lighthouse, and we even managed to move our pitch for one that had a sea view. There was also time to examine the maps and work out some plans for the days and weeks ahead, as we still had about seven weeks before we needed to get back to Sydney to celebrate Christmas with our family.

The local media was full of information about a partial eclipse that was due to take place, so on our second day I planned to get up early to watch. Unfortunately, in our rush to get away from Sydney and on the road, we hadn't bought batteries for our alarm clock so it failed to go off! I must have been partially awake though because as I lay there dozing lightly, I heard everything outside go quiet as the birds stopped their dawn chorus when the sky darkened, only to start again a few minutes later. A rare experience that I missed.

We left the site at 9.30 a.m., but not before a young English backpacker couple, about to give back their hired motorhome before returning home, gave us some food and a couple of champagne glasses. This was not an uncommon experience as people needed to clear their hired motorhomes before heading home and either gave away their perishables and other items they weren't taking with them, or left them in the camp kitchen for whoever wanted them.

First stop was a windscreen repair shop, where they fitted a new rubber surround to our windscreen, and then it was back to the main road, and before long we crossed into Queensland.

Bureaucracy

It was time to contact the agent, Bob Purdy, recommended to us by the Sydney RV Centre, to complete the administrative requirements and become 'official' owners of Matilda. We made contact by phone but he advised us he would be away for a few days and his assistant, Ferris, would help us out and take us through the process. It was only a short drive from Byron to Molendinar near Southport on the Gold Coast where we would meet Ferris, so first we made sure we knew where to meet up and then looked for a campsite for the night. For this, we made our way into Southport and arranged to stay a couple of nights at a campsite alongside the lagoon, and had a leisurely afternoon.

A hectic but frustrating day followed. We met Ferris as arranged at 9.00 a.m. at Bob Purdy's yard but waited an hour for the MOT engineer to arrive. He spent 45 minutes going over Matilda and found two things not to his liking. One, a frayed joint on one of the LPG pipes, was not an issue as we were able to repair it there and then. The other issue was the extra pair of wheels to the lazy axle that were non-standard. The inspector wasn't familiar with the design of the rear suspension with its extra axle and wouldn't pass it without seeing the original design drawings and engineering calculations. There was no chance of getting information about these as the company that built Matilda had gone out of business many years previously, and lodging an appeal against the engineer's decision could take a week to sort out, time we didn't want to waste. Our future travels were in jeopardy.

Ferris didn't want to let us down so we embarked on a tour of local suspension workshops to seek the opinion of others. We motored from one trading estate to another, trying to keep up with

Ferris in his own rather more nimble 4x4, with engineers coming out to crawl under Matilda, scratch their chins to ponder our problem and whether or not the suspension was adequate.

Some wouldn't commit, others thought it was alright, but even after a short break for lunch, we were still in limbo with no pass certificate which we could take to the local vehicle registration office, which closed at 3.30 p.m.

By 2.30 p.m., Ferris was getting desperate, so he decided the best bet was to take us to a mate of his who had a workshop and was authorised to carry out the inspections, and effectively we threw a six and started the process again. Within half an hour, the new inspector passed Matilda, and also retested the LPG system that we had repaired ourselves. He issued the necessary certificate and we whizzed out of the workshop to get to the vehicle registration office before it closed.

We did it with minutes to spare and after paying various fees and taxes, we had Matilda registered in our name: we breathed a sigh of relief. It was also time to head for a bar and buy Ferris a drink after which we headed back to the campsite and, later, went out for a pizza, at what turned out to be a brilliant Italian restaurant, to celebrate.

The next day it was time to head on again, and we were pleased to say goodbye to the Gold Coast. Southport and its neighbouring resort of Surfers Paradise were busy tourist spots with lots of foreign, mainly Asian, students and it wasn't our cup of tea at all. Similarly we had no intention of visiting Brisbane so kept to the main road bypassing it altogether.

Soon after we began to see signs to Australia Zoo, Steve Irwin's base, now being run by his wife following his sad death from a stingray sting when filming underwater off the Great Barrier Reef. We nearly turned off to visit the zoo, but decided to press on and were glad we did for we had an unexpected treat a few hours later.

Loggerhead turtle egg laying

Bundaberg is a major town, famous for its rum, and we decided it would be our next stopover. We went straight for the Visitor Information Centre where we learned that, for the first time this season, loggerhead turtles would probably be laying their eggs at a nearby beach that evening. We booked straight away and then headed to Bargara on the coast and checked into the campsite, had a hasty meal and went out again to nearby Burram Heads NP. The car park was busy and clearly a lot of people were hoping to see the egg laying too, but we all gathered in a small open-air amphitheatre for a briefing and instructional video. We were then split into groups and awaited word from the nearby beach that turtles were arriving: there was no guarantee.

It was now dark and we waited an hour. Another group was called forward and were guided off down a path towards the beach, and then another group and we began to wonder whether we would be lucky. Fortunately, at about 9.30 p.m., we were called and walked in complete darkness, apart from some dull red lighting, to the beach and as our eyes adjusted to the low light, we walked about half a mile to where a loggerhead turtle had just arrived on the beach.

There were two guides and about 30 people in our group, and we formed a circle around 'our' turtle to await some action.

The guides recognised this loggerhead as one they had christened Leila. She had been to this beach six or seven times before and was considered a mature and experienced female. Her carapace was a reddish-brown and she was about 5ft long, 3ft wide and probably weighed about 300 lbs.

Like so many of the Earth's creatures, the loggerhead is a threatened species. It is affected by pollution of the seas, its shell and meat is a delicacy in some parts of the world, and its eggs are a food source for scavengers. In Australia, loggerheads have been seriously affected by the red fox, introduced by the British for hunting purposes, which digs up their eggs as a food source.

Leila would probably lay about 1,000 eggs in her lifetime, but few of the tiny turtles, that would take eight weeks to hatch, were likely to make it to adulthood. The majority would be picked up by birds or become food to other marine life.

Behind us the surf lapped the beach and the moon shone, picking out the disturbed sand where our turtle had made her way up from the sea.

We waited at least another hour before the main action started as Leila began to dig out a hole for her eggs with her front flippers. After a brief rest, she then turned around and started to lay her white eggs, which dropped one by one into the hole. It was a fascinating sight, although in the semi-gloom with so many people standing around, one felt it was all a bit voyeuristic. However, it was nature and life in the raw, a wild creature doing what comes naturally to ensure that future generations of loggerhead turtles would be able to return and do exactly the same.

We spent a long evening watching this loggerhead turtle laying her eggs near Bundaberg, QLD

Another hour passed with more than a few people giving up and leaving to wander away, either through boredom or cold. Finally our turtle finished and started covering the eggs with her rear flippers and, after another breather, headed off down the beach and vanished into the sea. Leila had ignored the crowd around her and this last part reminded me of the end of the book and film *The Life of Pi*. The tiger that had threatened and harassed Pi throughout his lonely voyage just ups and blithely walks off into the jungle at the end of their voyage without any ceremony. Leila did the same. There was no acknowledgement that humans had been watching her for a couple of hours and that she was the centre of a lot of attention; she just upped and trudged off into the surf where she would wander the oceans for many months before seeing land again.

We were delighted with what we had seen, but there was more to come. The guides weren't happy with the site chosen by Leila as it was below the waterline at high tide which meant that the temperature generated in the clutch of eggs would be insufficient for them to hatch. They had to be moved, so they were dug up and counted very carefully, and then those people that were still present helped move all 161 eggs to a new hole higher up amongst the low dunes. A special treat indeed and we were able to handle many eggs, about the size of a ping pong ball but much more delicate.

It was well past midnight by the time we got back to the campsite but we were thrilled to have witnessed such a scene, and so early in our adventure. Hopefully there would be more to come.

With our late night, it was a slow start in the morning and we chose to travel a back road via Yandara. We needed to stop for fuel in Rosedale, a typical small, rural community; that was a treat. We turned off the road and crossed a narrow, wooden, humpbacked bridge over a railway line and found a village green and a small shop with a trio of ancient fuel pumps outside – it could so easily have been England in the 1940s, a real time warp of a place.

Matilda fails us

With Matilda running smoothly, we motored on and rejoined Route 1, and soon we arrived in Rockhampton. We found a campsite and parked up for the night, and as it was getting really warm, had a refreshing swim in the campsite pool.

By now we were getting used to the social side of travelling the roads, and on this evening we were invited to join a couple of retired teachers for a drink and some nibbles, and just as we were interested to hear about their travels, they were wanting to know more about our plans, and motorhoming in the UK and Europe.

In the morning, we packed up ready to go. Pam concentrated on the inside of Matilda, making sure everything was firmly put away, while I tackled the outside jobs – emptying the toilet cassette, coiling and stowing away the electrical hook-up cable and the waste water pipe, and making sure everything was closed and locked up.

We were ready to go so I turned the ignition key to start up Matilda – nothing. I tried again – another nothing, and nothing happened a few more times. With the bonnet up, there seemed to be nothing amiss, but no amount of trying would generate any spark at all.

I had noticed a motor accessory shop across the road from the campsite so after checking they had the right equipment, I carried the battery over there (in the mid-morning heat!) and they tested it, only to tell me it was dead and a replacement would be needed.

This would be a warranty item, so I needed to check with Sydney RV Centre that they would cover the cost, but it was Sunday, so we sat out the day and enjoyed more company with our teacher friends.

I had joined the equivalent of the AA/RAC which in Australia is the National Roads and Motorists' Association (NRMA), so phoned them up and arranged for an emergency crew to come out to us and get Matilda started with jump leads. We then ran it on a fast tick over for a while to build up a battery charge for her to start in the morning.

The mechanic also recommended a couple of electrical engineers in town.

The next day we headed off into town and soon found a place that could check Matilda that morning so left it with them and wandered over the road to an air-conditioned shopping mall and whiled away the morning.

We collected Matilda at lunchtime, by which time she had a new battery, but we were told she also needed a new water pump for the domestic side of the systems. As we drove away, we also noticed that the reversing camera had stopped working. More phone calls to Sydney RV Centre were made and they arranged for us to visit a motorhome repair place up the coast a bit near Mackay, where we were heading anyway.

We drove to Bakers Creek, about 250 km (150 miles), found the repair shop, made ourselves known to the mechanics and arranged to call back in the morning for the additional repairs to be made. For a campsite, they suggested the General Gordon public house in Homebush, about 16 km (10 miles) away, so off we went.

We easily found the pub; it was surrounded by sugar cane fields where there was a lot of activity. The sugar cane grows very quickly and is harvested and loaded onto small rail trucks which are pulled by little diesel locomotives on miles and miles of light railway system to refineries. These trains were coming and going and were fed by a fleet of lorries loaded high with cane.

The pub looked a bit scruffy and run-down but we checked in anyway and were told we could camp at the back on an open area and use the bathroom facilities on the upper floor of the building.

We set up for the night. There was no electricity, and I went up the outside staircase to examine the facilities. On the typical Australian open balcony, I found the toilet/shower – very dirty and dilapidated: there was no way we would use it. I checked out some of the rooms and they were filthy dives, only suitable for desperate backpackers.

Later we went into the pub and as there were some locals eating, we thought we would risk a meal. Like most Australian pubs, the bar was an eclectic mix of historic photos and memorabilia, together with more modern adornments such as flags, and this one even had a wooden bicycle hanging from the ceiling.

Standard fare in the pubs is meat and veg – often huge slabs of meat sitting on a pile of potatoes, carrot, cauliflower, corn, peas and more; a big plateful for big appetites and usually great grub. We took our meal with some beer out into a large open lean-to at the side of the pub and ate while chatting to a local family sitting at a nearby table. Suddenly Pam cried out as she spotted a rat scuttling across the floor and disappearing behind a screen. Not a frequent sight in British pubs!

We finished the meal and, when chatting with the landlady afterwards, asked about the rat and local wildlife in general.

"Oh, you'll get a lot of water rats at present as they're working the cane fields tonight and they get disturbed."

"Really? Anything else likely to be about?" I asked.

"Well, the brown snakes and taipans eat the rats and they will soon be along as well. We had a brown in the kitchen the other day, and often get taipans in the cellar." Browns and taipans are the two most venomous snakes on the planet!

"Will we see them tonight?" I tentatively asked.

"Probably not. But to be sure, use your torch when you walk back to your motorhome." Oh boy!

We most certainly did use a torch – and fortunately we didn't see anything. However we were kept up most of the night as the work in the adjacent cane fields continued without stopping. There were big lighting rigs set up, lorries chuntering about and, from time to time, little diesel engines shunting their trucks into position and pulling them away to the refinery.

Inevitably there were cane toads around. Australia's problem with cane toads is fairly well known and dates back to the 1930s when Queensland's cane farmers were having problems with the Frenchi cane beetle and the greyback beetle attacking their crops. Scientists had heard that the introduction of cane toads in Hawaii had been successful in increasing the crop of sugar cane there, so why not in Australia?

Scientific knowledge was far less than it is today and we are talking about a time before DDT was in use to control pests, so Reginald Mungomery, the scientist involved, was instrumental in importing an initial batch of about 100 toads with the aim of dealing with the beetle problems in Queensland.

All went well for a while and a year later a further 60,000 toads were released across the affected countryside – and then the problems started. Cane toads are prolific breeders and their numbers increased rapidly. However, they weren't very good at dealing with the beetle problem. The beetles lived at the top of cane plants, which are rather taller in Australia than in other countries, and the toads were found to be poor climbers.

The beetles remained but the cane toads thrived and started to affect various indigenous species as the skin of the toads is covered with a toxic slime. When they are attacked by natural predators such as lizards and snakes, creatures that have no natural resistance to the new toxin, they fall sick and die. But the toads continue to thrive and are now endemic across northern Australia from Brisbane to Darwin; and they, no doubt, will spread further west if a control measure is not found.

Needless to say, a great deal of effort is being made to find a solution to the problem, but poor old Mungomery gets the blame for what seemed to be a good plan at the time.

We were at the motorhome workshop at 9.00 a.m. prompt, and within half an hour we were given a cup of coffee and the mechanics were busy working on Matilda. They were very friendly and chatty and plied us with coffee (as there was nowhere to go), and by lunchtime they had finished what they could. In addition to doing the reversing camera and water pump repairs, they checked out the air conditioning in the accommodation and did a small repair, and noted the system in the cab, as fitted originally in the Toyota, was working below par. They recommended someone in nearby Mackay who would be able to fix it.

Whilst I had expected some warranty work might be needed on Matilda, I was getting a bit fed up with the scope of the work, and the time it was taking to get it sorted out. I knew we weren't paying for it, but nevertheless I felt some of the shortcomings we had uncovered should have been found in a decent pre-delivery check. I expressed my concerns to the general manager of Sydney RV Centre who was very apologetic and assured us that anything else would be covered, just let him know. He missed the point rather, as it was the time it was taking out of our trip and the worry that something more serious might go wrong when we were off the beaten track and which might leave us stranded in the middle of nowhere.

We had learned a bit about the history of the Matilda models over the last few days from various people we had spoken to. They had originally been designed and constructed by a Cairns boat builder who had been one of the first in Australia to apply the techniques of fibreglass used in boat building to the construction of motorhomes. This meant that surfaces were smooth and easy to clean, and one didn't have the many joints that conventional construction techniques for motorhomes usually have.

Several variations of the Matilda model had been built; a shorter wheelbase version without the extra wheels, as well as two-wheel drive versions of both sizes.

However, a big problem arose for those that had bought the various Matilda models as it seems Toyota weren't being paid for the Hilux chassis they were supplying. Toyota obtained a court order to seize all the existing stock and, most unusually, those that had been sold. The huge furore that followed meant that the seized vehicles were stored for many years before finding their way back onto the market. Ours, it seems, was one of those.

Nevertheless Matilda was growing on us and we were beginning to like her. She ran nicely, had all the facilities on board that we wanted for our extended trip, and her off-road potential seemed good.

After some lunch in Mackay, we found the air conditioning specialist and he started checking behind the dashboard, only to find a nest of dried grass and twigs. In addition, the fan showed signs of gnawing and between us we decided it had probably been a rat's nest at some time in the past. Another call to Sydney RV Centre and a major moan followed. The whole area behind the dashboard and glove box was cleaned out, the air conditioning filters cleaned out too, and a solenoid was replaced. Eventually we were on the road again and headed 200 km (120 miles) to Bowen, and camping at a beachside site close to a lovely little bay and café at Horseshoe Harbour.

With all the stops for repairs, it was time to take stock and decide where we might head to next. We wanted to visit the Great Barrier Reef and had planned to do so at Cairns, still several hundred miles away. I also wanted to go inland and do some serious off-road mileage, possibly the Birdsville Track in the deep, south-east of Queensland, but needed some off-road mileage near civilisation first in case we encountered problems with Matilda.

Whitsunday Islands

We sat and enjoyed Horseshoe Harbour the next day and had a leisurely lunch in a little café while we hatched a plan. We would take a trip to the Whitsunday Islands from Airlie Beach, a little south of where we were now, and then head back to Bowen and then west down the gravel Bowen Developmental Road. Someone had told us it was relatively smooth and they had taken their standard caravan down it with an ordinary road car.

Fully refreshed, the next day we headed back from where we had come and turned towards the coast to Airlie Beach, a busy tourist town that considers itself to be the gateway to the Whitsunday Islands. The Islands are very popular with the sailing fraternity and the archipelago hosts several upmarket holiday resorts on its islands. As they are at the southern end of the Great Barrier Reef, there is plenty of coral to see.

We booked a one-day trip on an inflatable that included some snorkelling, lunch and a visit to the beautiful Whitehaven Beach. There were about 20 people on the boat with a couple of crew and we were by far the oldest. By chance we happened to sit next to a couple of English lasses on a short trip to Australia who worked in our local police headquarters. Needless to say, they were more interested in the lads on board than talking to us old fogeys.

We sailed away from Airlie Beach and soon stopped for our first swim. We had anchored in a small bay and once we were kitted out with stinger suits (to minimise the effects of stings from any lurking jellyfish), a mask and snorkel, we jumped in and had a half hour swim amongst the coral and multi-coloured fish.

We headed on around the islands and eventually reached Whitehaven Beach where we disembarked onto the soft, white sand that is 98% pure silica, and walked across the foreshore and up a hill to a viewing spot. The view across the bay and up an inlet was gorgeous with the white sands stretching away into the distance and the lush green foliage acting as a backdrop. It is a much photographed view regularly seen in holiday brochures.

By the time we got back to the raft, an alfresco lunch was ready so we had a lazy couple of hours enjoying lunch and then swimming in a warm tidal pool accompanied by small stingrays whizzing about and diving into the sand. This was as close to nirvana I had ever been – it was a simply gorgeous experience.

On the way back to Airlie Beach, we stopped at another snorkelling spot and saw more coral and fishes and then it was back to base. A beautiful day in paradise: who would want to head on?

Tempting as it was to spend more time in the area, we needed to press on. We started a new phase of the trip by driving back to Bowen and heading inland and onto gravel roads into the Outback.

"At the end of my trial,
I was rather hoping the judge would send me
to Australia for the rest of my life."

Jeffrey Archer
(Author)

Part 3

* Into the Outback
* Christmas in November
* Longreach
* Middleton Hilton Hotel
* Disney in the desert
* Birdsville
* Birdsville Track on our own
* Marree
* Murder on a quiet afternoon
* R&R in Semaphore
* Victor Harbor
* Heading back east
* Bendigo
* Matilda races round Mount Panorama
* Back into Sydney

Into the Outback

The Bowen Development Road heads south-west from Bowen and the first third of the road was unexpectedly tarmac so we made quick progress to Collinsville for a coffee stop. Leaving town, the road turned to gravel and the next 160 km (100 miles) were on a well-maintained track passing a couple of opencast coal mines on the way.

As we left the coastal region, the land became more arid and a plume of dust followed us as Matilda bowled along at about 80 kph (50 mph). We had become a bit worried about her because of the problems we had had, but she was built for this sort of travel and was now in her element. The suspension was sound, the tyres gripped well, she steered adequately and took to it all like a duck to water. I was enjoying the drive as well and the track twisted this way and that, and there were numerous dried-up creeks to cross. These were anything from three to fifteen feet deep and whilst there was usually a warning sign, we needed to slow right down and drop down into the creek bed, and then climb out on the other side and pick up speed again.

I suppose we were fortunate in that in the whole of our time in Australia, we rarely had any rain, just the odd few days here and there; the worst was already behind us, but the lack of water in the creeks was indicative of the drought problems that Australia suffers.

We were prepared for water; engine electrics had had a good dose of WD40 and Matilda had a snorkel as well, so in theory we could have driven through at least three feet of water, as I have done in the past, but it was not to be on this trip. However, I definitely believe in being prepared!

We also saw some wildlife on the road, a few blue-tongue lizards scuttling away as we approached and a few kangaroos, our first on this trip, including a huge male that must have stood seven feet tall.

Blue-tongue lizards really do have blue tongues,
as seen at the Reptile Centre, Alice Springs, NT

There was also some other traffic. A couple of 4x4s came the other way as well as some road trains with a string of trailers loaded with mining equipment. We knew we had to be very wary of these juggernauts as they give way to nobody. The rule is to get as far over to the left as possible, often right off the road in the bush, stop, and let them pass. The main danger is from flying stones.

We reached the end of the track without incident and hit a sealed road that took us a few miles into a roadhouse at Belyando Crossing. We were now on Route 55, an alternative main north/south road in eastern Australia, which attracts a lot of lorry traffic. Belyando Crossing was the equivalent of a motorway service area in the UK; it offered fuel, food and refreshments, a huge pull-off area for lorries, some basic accommodation, and a small campsite at the back. However, it was the only stopping place between Charters Towers, 210 km (131 miles) to the north, and Clermont, 200 km (120 miles) to the south. In between, the only turnings off the main road were to cattle stations, and often these were many miles away.

We got fuel, booked an overnight stay and drove round to the campsite. The first thing that was obvious to us was the covering of dust over the inside of Matilda, dust that had been kicked up as we drove down the track and been blown inside. We decided that as soon as possible, we would get some large plastic bags and store some of our vulnerable belongings, such as bedding and my laptop, in them.

Christmas in November

There were a couple of caravans and motorhomes in the campsite already and, as we chose our spot, a young guy with a tinnie in his hand and an Esky at his side gave us a wave and invited us over for a drink. For the uninitiated, an Esky is an insulated cool box, usually blue and white, and essential kit for the Australian drinking culture.

We set up Matilda for the night, grabbed a couple of our own tinnies, and wandered over to join our new friend. James was good company, explaining that he was camping with his wife, Amy, her sister, Jessie, and her partner, Craig, plus the girls' mum and dad. The three couples were meeting up as a Christmas get-together because they would all be busy with other family commitments on 25th December. The six of them all lived in various parts of Queensland and this was a central point for a celebration together. Never mind that it was only 24th November – this was Australia!

One thing led to another and as they had all brought plenty of Christmas food, they insisted we join them. What an evening we had, although before we ate we had a slightly embarrassing few minutes. It was, after all, Christmas so they exchanged Christmas presents together with lots of hugging and kissing, just what one might expect at a family celebration. There were crackers to pull and decorations were draped around their awning; apart from the Australian heat and being in shorts, it was all very Christmassy.

Everyone toasted everyone else and they did a special toast to their Pommie guests; we returned the compliment, of course. We could only contribute some crisps and beers to the evening, but out of a tiny camping trailer, the mother, Leonie, and the girls produced all manner of fine foods – prawns, lamb, sausages, and salads all followed by terrific sweets, and more and more alcohol. It was tough, but eventually we rolled, almost literally, back to Matilda very late and slept well into the following morning.

We had experienced terrific Australian hospitality from an open and friendly family and been welcomed into their fold without any hesitation. It was the first of several such incidents and we rarely had anything but complete friendliness from our Australian hosts.

In the morning, with sore heads we bade farewell to our new friends and headed off once more. We followed the main road south to Clermont, before finding a side turning and went agricultural again down another gravel track, eventually to Alpha.

This track was about 200 km (120 miles), sometimes with narrow stretches of tarmac, and every so often there were side turnings leading away to distant cattle stations. We passed signposts to places such as Surbiton and Malden, presumably named when they were first established, after the home towns of the first settlers in the region. We both knew these London suburbs well; in fact, Pam was brought up in Malden.

Roughly halfway along this track was a surprise. We had seen occasional signs warning of the presence of school buses and then seemingly in the middle of nowhere was a school; life is very different out here. We would have stopped at the school to investigate but it was a Sunday and there was nobody around.

At Alpha, a small town on the Capricorn Highway, so named as it lies alongside the Tropic of Capricorn, we found a rather run-down and basic campsite, and started to deal with the new shortcoming we had found with Matilda. Dust. It would become the bane of our lives when travelling on the remote tracks. Matilda might take them in her stride, but she wasn't dust proof, and there was plenty of red dust about. It got everywhere, especially in the cupboards over the wheel arches and in the coming months we would spend many an hour cleaning it all out.

Overnight we suffered a bit from lorry noise as there was a major road junction nearby and road trains would be obliged to stop before turning and building up speed again as they headed west on the Capricorn Highway, a main route from the east coast towards Alice Springs and Darwin in the Northern Territories.

There was nothing to keep us in the morning so we joined the road trains heading west and stopped at Barcaldine, a town with a bit of history. The town saw the birth of the Australian Labour Party in 1891 when there was a strike by local sheep shearers. Over a thousand strikers wanting better pay and conditions gathered in front of the railway station on 1st May under a ghost gum tree, something that became known as the Tree of Knowledge.

This tree is now a national monument to the Labour movement but an attack by vandals poisoned it and the tree died, to be replaced by a strange edifice. Outside the station there now stands a huge metal structure held up by four corner posts and a corrugated roof, and underneath hangs dozens of wooden poles. The remnants of the original tree are also preserved.

It was getting very hot and the daytime temperature was well above 35C, very warm for Brits, so we paid a visit to a pub for some cold beer. The young bartender told us of some of the problems in the area, mainly resulting from a continued drought. The town, he felt, was dying on its feet and there were currently five hotels, none of which were making any money, and really there was only a need for one. There was little to attract people to the town, and other than a stop for fuel, people just drove through. This was a story we would hear several times, as many small country towns seemed to struggle in the modern era. Like so many parts of the world, youngsters want more than can be offered in small town Australia and with the offer of better jobs and opportunities in the cities, they move away. Gradually a town withers as essential community services and commercial activities close. The huge mining boom in Australia has also contributed to this effect, and the chance of good salaries in coal, uranium, gold and other mines is a great draw. Tourism often offers the main chance for these towns to flourish, and our next destination, Longreach, had plenty on offer.

Longreach

As usual, we drove straight to the Visitor Information Centre and the outside temperature was posted on a board – 38C (100.4F). It was baking hot and we were struggling to acclimatise. We managed to find a shady spot for Matilda but even the walk over the road to the centre was a chore.

Research before leaving the UK advised us of three possible attractions in the town. QANTAS, the Australian national airline, had started up near here, and a dedicated heritage centre had been established with various aircraft on display.

Nearby was another visitor attraction dedicated to the pioneering stockmen who established the pastoral practices in this part of rural Queensland, and finally there was a School of the Air to visit.

A handwritten whiteboard notice advised of a meeting of Longreach Lions Club that evening, and as a member of my local Lions Club in Guildford, I wanted to know more.

Lions Clubs International is an international organisation of volunteers raising money to give to charitable causes and doing other activities to help their communities. Lions are always welcome at other clubs. There are 40,000 across the world, and in my travels I have been to Lions Clubs in South America when there on an extended trip, as well as a couple of visits to Manly Lions Club in Sydney.

We checked into the campsite, which was very large, but almost empty with just a few caravans and motorhomes parked up in the dusty pitches, all under as much shade as they could find. We found a friendly tree as well and the heat meant it would be the first time we would run the air conditioning all night.

I thought it would be interesting to visit the Lions Club meeting so made contact with the club secretary and later joined about 15 of their members at a local hotel for an evening meal, the usual massive plate of meat and veg which made me sweat like a pig. I was made very welcome, and just as I was keen to know about their club, they wanted to know about my experiences in a UK Lions Club.

Back at the campsite later in the evening, the temperature didn't drop below 30C, so to make sleeping more comfortable, I left Pam to sleep on the bed over the cab, whilst I moved to the rear double instead. In fact, this arrangement continued for the rest of the trip.

The night time temperature didn't drop below 30C for most of the next week, but gradually we became a little more used to it, and adjusted our activities accordingly.

We pulled out our awning so as to create a bit more shade, but during the night the wind blew up and I had to creep out and roll it back just in case it came loose.

I guess like most people I learned about the Australian School of the Air during my own education. With small, remote communities and cattle stations often hundreds of miles from anywhere significant, the School of the Air was started up using basic radio sets to communicate with children from a central location and provide them with an education. Gradually, as technology has improved, treadle operated radios have given way to more modern forms of communication, and now email, the internet and Skype services have made the process much more flexible.

The School of the Air in Longreach, or more properly the Longreach School of Distance Education (LSODE), was just one of several schools around Australia providing a comprehensive education service for hundreds of children living in remote locations. Unfortunately for us, it was holiday time for the children so there were no lessons in progress but on our visit a very well informed guide gave us a tour of the school and its facilities.

The school had over 150 pupils, most in Queensland although some were in the Northern Territories and New South Wales. As one might expect, there are all manner of unusual problems. Some children have parents who are itinerant workers and keeping track of them can be very difficult, even getting to the stations to visit the children can be an adventure as the roads may be in poor condition, flooded, or even closed.

Because it is important for the children to interact with each other and their teachers, the school also brings them into Longreach and there are dormitories for them to stay in, and have lessons and play in a conventional school setting.

The QANTAS Founders Centre was only about half a mile away, but there was no way we were going to walk there – it was simply too hot. We drove round, parked up beside a Boeing 747 and walked into the air-conditioned reception as quickly as possible.

QANTAS, which stands for Queensland and Northern Territories Aerial Service, started up near Longreach in the 1920s and has gradually grown into the major international airline we know today.

In addition to touring the exhibits, most of which were, fortunately, inside air-conditioned buildings, we also booked to take a look at the aircraft on display outside, and being a very quiet time of year we were the only people, together with a chap from Cairns. He had flown a pal to Longreach for a business appointment in his small private plane and was just filling time. He would be flying back in the morning, leaving early to take advantage of the still air at that time of day.

The guide took us into the 747, named the *City of Bunbury*, after a city in Western Australia, south of Perth. During its time, it had travelled 130 million kilometres (82 million miles), the equivalent of flying to the moon and back ten times, and had carried over five million passengers. When it was first proposed that it should be displayed at Longreach, there was great consternation in the town about whether it would actually be able to land at the modest airport as the runway was never designed for such a huge aircraft. However, on the day all went well and it seemed to me to be in fine condition and a worthy part of the centre.

After a tour inside and a sit in the pilot's seat, we were shown the so-called 'black' boxes set high up in the ceiling under the tail fin, the safest part of an aircraft and the section of a plane most likely to remain intact in case of a crash.

Next we had our photo taken as we stood inside the engine intake cowl of one of the four Rolls Royce engines, before heading into the next plane, a Boeing 707.

This one had been the first jet flown by QANTAS and, after many years of service, was sold and served other airlines and some private operators. Supposedly these included Michael Jackson, Madonna, and some Arab sheikhs. Eventually the plane was left abondoned at Southend Airport in Essex, UK but was recovered, made airworthy and flown back to Australia to become part of the museum.

Whilst the plane was painted in QANTAS colours, the inside was still arranged as it had been for private use. It was fitted out with a lot of hardwood; bedrooms and lounges were lined with fancy woods and there were cabinets storing cut crystal glass. The bathroom was as good as anyone might find in a smart hotel.

The next day we headed for the Stockman's Hall of Fame based in a striking, modern building opened by Queen Elizabeth II in 1988. In fact Prince Charles and the Duchess of Cornwall (Camilla) had visited Longreach and the Hall of Fame only a couple of weeks before we got there.

The harshness of life in the Australian Outback was very cleverly portrayed in a series of displays incorporating new technology alongside appropriate memorabilia and artefacts. We were travelling the Outback in air-conditioned splendour, but the life led by the original settlers must have been very hard.

Back at the campsite, we got talking to some Australians camping nearby. They were a couple in their mid-thirties with three children aged between eight and fourteen, and were living in a tiny camping trailer towed by a Toyota Prado (sold as a Colorado in the UK). They had been on the road, almost permanently, for five years, educating their children with help from their home state education service, picking up work from time to time. They were so well organised having to live in such a small space, but the children were having a fantastic educational experience and seemed to be thriving on it. Such a practice is not too unusual in Australia and the education authorities support such trips and help the parents with continuing educational support. As we had found at the School of the Air, the internet and email help.

Before we left Longreach, we had some major decisions to make. Although the town lies on the main road from the populated east coast to Mount Isa and thence to Alice Springs and Darwin, the region to the south-west was more remote than we had encountered so far. Our plan was to head to Birdsville, in the very south-west corner of Queensland, nearly 800 km (500 miles) away along remote and little travelled highways, much of which would be gravel roads. From Birdsville, we would then head down the Birdsville Track, another 504 km (315 miles) to Marree with virtually no habitation of any kind along the way. Then we aimed to head south and it would still be lonely roads until we reached more populated areas north of Adelaide.

So we could bale out now and head back east via a variety of routes, or we could head on as planned and have another escape opportunity at Birdsville where there were other options to return east, should we need them.

In coming to these decisions over the last couple of weeks, I had been carrying out checks on our fuel consumption, both petrol and LPG, and although we had been mostly on tarmac roads, I was satisfied we would be alright, provided we hit no serious and lengthy patches of water or mud, both of which would reduce fuel consumption rapidly. We made numerous enquiries around town and decided to press on, at least to Birdsville.

The road to Winton, about 177 km (111 miles) was a sealed main road and posed no problems, except the heat which was winding up and was now well over 40C. Winton was the spiritual home of our own temporary home, Matilda, as a local poet, Barton 'Banjo' Paterson, wrote the famous bush ballad *Waltzing Matilda* nearby. The first public performance took place in the town in 1895 and the ballad is now the unofficial national anthem of the nation.

We stopped for refreshment in a coffee shop and the heat was blistering, far higher than anything we had ever encountered before, and we have both been to many warm climes. The streets were empty and anyone with any business in town soon darted into an air-conditioned building from their air-conditioned vehicle.

Next we headed west on the Kennedy Developmental Highway towards Boulia 380 km (240 miles) away, a single track road I had expected to be mostly gravel but had been improved with the installation of tarmac, so the going was pretty easy.

Middleton Hilton Hotel

We were, however, heading into more remote territory. The land was very arid, almost virtually flat, and had little vegetation. Either side of the highway, we could see occasional cattle and the odd acacia tree, but otherwise there was little to attract the eye.

Traffic was almost nil. Over the 200 km (120 miles) to the Middleton Hotel, we came across one road train heading the opposite way. Fortunately, one can see these behemoths from far away and we knew that they stop for no one and hug the centre line of the road. It would be up to us to pull over onto the verge, slow down or stop, and let him pass by before picking up our own speed again. This was fine in dry weather, but had it been wet, the verge may well have been soft and muddy and then all manner of problems can, and do, arise.

Along the way, we passed just one cattle station, at Woodstock, otherwise there was nothing until we reached Middleton in the mid-afternoon.

The community here had been established in the 1860s during the days of the old horse-drawn coaching routes, Middleton being a place where the horses were changed, refreshments obtained, and accommodation provided. Cobb & Co. was the major carrier throughout much of Australia and various towns still displayed old Cobb & Co. coaches; Middleton had one too. But there wasn't much else except a very dilapidated corrugated iron village hall and the remnants of an old horse racing track.

The roadhouse itself lay on the north side of the road and opposite was the Middleton Hilton, a dusty parking area with a small structure offering a bit of shade for anyone sitting under it. Many years ago, some wag had erected a notice *Hilton Hotel* on this structure and for ever more it has become the Hilton, and well known amongst the RV and backpacker fraternity.

When planning our adventure, we had considered having the odd hotel stay as we made our way round Australia, and I knew about the Middleton Hilton so had been promising Pam a stay in a Hilton, something she was starting to look forward to. She soon caught on.

We parked up and our priority was a couple of cold beers, so it was straight to the bar. To be honest, the place was very scruffy and run-down. It was surrounded by a range of derelict sheds and enclosures, and a few small paddocks with some animals, including a pet camel and, somewhat incongruously, a bright blue Robinson two-seater helicopter. The hotel was run by an elderly couple, their son and his family, and in the evening there were a few locals around who proved to be great company. We were informed that the son of the family was the pilot and used the helicopter for rounding up cattle, and was, supposedly, a dab hand at unlocking and locking paddock gates without landing!

Later, Grandma cooked us a meal and was proud to show us some fossils she had picked up over the years in the environs. She told us her family had emigrated as £10 Poms from Haslemere in Surrey, just down the road from where we live. Middleton was very different to Surrey!

Grandad had a fund of amusing stories and poems, none of which can be repeated here; in Pam's diary, she described them as 'male humour'.

The meal was good, plain cooking, and very enjoyable, and we then sat on the veranda with Grandad and some of his cronies, drinking tinnies. Middleton was not for the fashion conscious as dirty vests and tatty shorts seemed to be the order of the day, together with a week's growth on the chin. However, they were real characters working at wrangling cattle and fossicking (searching for gem stones) when they couldn't find other work.

One asked me, "Where did you say you were from?"

"From the UK."

"And how long have you been over here in Australia?"

"About two months."

"You know, if your great grandad had done more thieving, you'd have been here ages ago."

Typical Australian humour, and later in the evening, we started talking about crocodiles.

"Have you seen any crocodiles yet?" asked one of the guys.

"Not yet," I replied. "I guess we will see some once we get into the Top End."

"You'll need to be careful not to go swimming in rivers and creeks, or even stand near the edge of the water – they will grab you, pull you over and go into a death roll."

"Yes, we've heard about that."

"Do you know what they call people who stand at the edge of slipways and go swimming where they shouldn't?"

"No."

"Bait."

And then they started talking about the Min Min. It seems that many people have experienced the Min Min, a strange light that is only seen rarely, but one that follows people around in the area between Middleton and Boulia. People can get pretty scared by the Min Min and numerous scientific minds have applied themselves to its origins, but no one has come up with a proper answer to its cause.

Of course, all these guys reckoned they had seen it, usually many years ago, and I think the light got bigger according to how many tinnies they had finished off.

Earlier we had also met Chloe, the granddaughter, a lass about ten years old, but who was very mature in her outlook and acted more like a 15-year-old. She was taught via the School of the Air and her nearest chum lived about 65 km (40 miles) away. It must be tough being brought up in such a remote location, with little contact with children her own age, but, as the LSODE told us, most of their students did better than conventionally schooled pupils.

One skill Chloe had in spades was in riding a motorbike and a quad. She sped around the area doing wheelies and sliding about, better than many experienced adults could. She told us she and her cousin were entered in a motorcycle competition in a couple of days' time at Bedourie, so we said we would try and be there.

In the morning, we awoke from our beds at the Hilton to find two of the guys we were chatting with last night laid out on the ground in swags, a combined groundsheet and sleeping bag that is very popular in Australia. They had slept out under the stars, something they probably did on most nights.

As we were getting ready to leave, the helicopter took off, and was flown about two feet off the road for about a quarter of a mile down the middle of the road before lifting up into the sky and away. Show off!

We left and continued our journey westward, coming across a couple more road trains and also red rocky outcrops (mesas) about 150ft tall with scree slopes leading to vertical sides and capped with flat tabletops.

We stopped at a lookout at Cawnpore to admire the view, and we could see the road meandering away in both directions for many miles.

It was stiflingly hot; we reckoned it must have been 45C (113F), but something that is all too common in this part of the world. Fortunately it was a dry heat; had it been humid as well, I doubt we would have gotten out of Matilda's air-conditioned interior.

This was lonely, isolated territory and we were now in Channel Country. Other than occasional, rocky outcrops such as we had seen, the land is very, very flat and this whole area of south-western Queensland, together with parts of neighbouring Northern Territories, South Australia, and New South Wales, are part of a huge river basin that, for most of the time, has little or no water.

Shallow, sinuous drainage channels flow south-west forming three river systems, the Diamentina and Georgina Rivers, and Coopers

Creek, eventually draining into Lake Eyre, a huge salt lake, more or less in the middle of the Australian continent.

The Channel Country is vast, covering about a sixth of the whole of Australia and rain, when it falls, in parts of northern Queensland, will flow south into this system. Australia, however, seems to suffer almost perpetual drought and the rivers only flow on rare occasions, and when they do, huge areas flood and road travel becomes all but impossible. Fortunately for us, conditions were dry, otherwise we probably wouldn't have tried heading this way.

Disney in the desert

It was a long and lonely drive to Boulia, a modest little town where we had a coffee and did some shopping in the only shop. Here they stocked everything from frozen food to chainsaws, and the shop assistant turned out to be a backpacker from Cardiff. It's very hard to recruit staff out here and backpackers are attracted by the offer of free accommodation, food, a salary, and more importantly, no attractions such as bars and nightlife. For her it was a good way of spending a few months getting some money together to fund her further travels.

We were right out in the boondocks, yet over the road was a novel attraction that reminded us of the very best Disney has to offer. The *Min Min Encounter Show* was themed around the famous light phenomena we had heard all about. It offered a 45 minute show with animatronic displays in various 'rooms' elaborating on bush yarns based on the ethereal light. It was so unexpected in such a remote location and we were blown away by it. Amazing!

It was still blisteringly hot, but before heading to a campsite I wanted to head out of town to check out the beginning of the Donohue Highway, one that heads west to end up not far from Alice Springs. I had no plans to tackle the track now, but had given it consideration for later on in our trip.

As we had found before, various signs at the start of these tracks offer plenty of warnings about the potential difficulties ahead, the distances involved and likely fuel availability. In particular, I noticed a sign indicating distances to various cattle stations that could be accessed along the 800 km (500 mile) track. It would be easy to misread them as, for example, it indicated that it was 114 km (71 miles) to Cravens Peak turn-off, and one might suppose that if one got stuck there, help might be close at hand. No. That was just the turn-off; the cattle station itself was a further 78 km (48 miles) – a long walk if you broke down. You would probably die from dehydration or sunstroke long before getting there.

At the campsite at the edge of town, we had a cold shower, and as we walked back to Matilda, a 5ft goanna (monitor lizard) wandered by. We had seen a couple from a distance as we drove along, but this was the first we had seen up close. It wasn't troubled by our presence and just wandered along sniffing here and there and swishing its tail back and forth.

It was 225 km (140 miles) to Bedourie the next day, mostly on a gravel track with the landscape still very flat and arid. Occasionally there were groups of cattle seemingly happy with their lot but clearly struggling to find food. Many of the cattle we had seen in recent weeks had their origins in European breeds, but increasingly, as the land became drier and more arid, we were seeing Brahman, a breed we associated with the Indian sub-continent, but which is ideally suited to the Australian Outback climate.

After getting fuel, we headed out along a very sandy track to the racecourse at Bedourie where the motorcycle event was being staged. It was an event for juniors and we watched Chloe beat several older boys in short, gymkhana style tests, having to ride her quad in a zigzag between posts, around and back to a finishing line. Elsewhere there were kids zooming around on their motorbikes testing themselves on small hillocks and jumps. Everyone seemed to be having a great time, except the family from Middleton. We found them at the bar, all looking dejected as they had brought a motorbike along for their son, and it had developed a serious mechanical problem on its first run, so the trip was very much wasted. Chloe seemed to be doing well, though, and enjoying herself.

It was too hot to sit around so we decided to climb back on board Matilda, switch on the air conditioning, and head on another 160 km (100 miles) to Birdsville.

Birdsville

Birdsville is an iconic destination in the Australian psyche, along with Uluru and Cape York. It is very isolated, and as we had found, it takes a lot of effort to get there and many adventurers have Birdsville on their bucket list. It had been on my list for a long time so I was able to give my list a big tick as we drove into town.

The town lies on the border with South Australia, and not too far from the Northern Territories border. We approached from the north, and there were three possible options away from here. To the west lies the Simpson Desert and a very sandy desert track over dozens of sand dunes, normally only tackled by expert 4x4 drivers. Getting stuck here, and getting back out, can cost a fortune, and many are caught out by the hazards the track has to offer. We had no plans to take Matilda that way: one, because we were travelling alone, two, we planned to head south, and three, because the track closed the day before we arrived for three months to 'recover'.

The other options out of town were to the east along more remote and isolated tracks to Windorah and on again towards New South Wales, an area I would like to visit if I ever get the chance to venture into the Outback again, or as we planned south down the Birdsville Track into South Australia.

Arriving in Birdsville, we headed straight to the petrol station and were told that the pumps were out of action because at 44.1C it was too hot and the pumps wouldn't work; could we come back in the morning when it was cooler? So we headed for the Birdsville Hotel for a couple of cold beers and to start collecting information on the condition of the track.

From the ever friendly crowd at the bar, we heard two stories that warn of the dangers ahead, and of travelling these parts in poorly prepared vehicles. Charlie and Bruce were two carpenters from Melbourne who had been at the hotel for a couple of days. Their boss in Melbourne had sent them in the company van to deliver some display cabinets to the Visitor Information Centre in Birdsville. They knew nothing about the track and headed up from Marree at the bottom end, and along the way had punctures on every tyre, including their spare. Somehow they had struggled into Birdsville and were now stuck, and bored out of their minds, until replacement tyres could be delivered from Mount Isa – maybe within the next week.

They were lucky, unlike the backpackers who had headed off down the track a couple of years previously. They had bought a dilapidated 4x4 in Darwin when they arrived in Australia and in complete innocence had taken to driving in the deserts. They had left Birdsville one morning to head south, but their vehicle broke down within an hour and they decided they could walk back to town for help. They quickly became dehydrated; one died whilst the other was rescued just in time.

They broke the cardinal rule of desert driving - if you break down, you stay with the vehicle, even if it takes days for help to arrive. One can survive on little or no food and some water for many days, but with no shade trying to walk any distance in the desert can be a death sentence.

When we were in Birdsville, we also heard of the recent tragic death of a station worker who left his vehicle when it became stuck in sand. Apparently two workers drove a well-equipped Hilux to a remote part of a local cattle station to carry out some maintenance work. It seems they didn't leave any information about what they were doing, how long they would be, or where they were heading.

On the return journey to the station, the vehicle got stuck in soft sand and for whatever reason they decided to walk 16 km back to their base. This was despite the fact that the vehicle had a high lift jack, a winch, and both men were experienced Outback workers. One man only made 6 km before dying, the other nearly died but was rescued.

NEVER leave your vehicle if it becomes stuck or breaks down in remote areas. Always carry sufficient water and food, tools, spare parts and communications equipment – and await rescue; someone will always be along in due course. In addition, let someone know where you are travelling and how long you anticipate being in the Outback.

Being midsummer, Birdsville was very quiet and we had the campsite to ourselves, which was fine until we went to use the facilities. They had been closed up for a couple of weeks so the electrics were off and I had to do a good search round with a torch to make sure there were no unwelcome visitors of the slithery kind.

The town might have been quiet for us, but the population of 300 people increases to several thousand when the main event of the year, the Birdsville Races, take place each September. Then there can be 500 light aircraft parked up in the little airport with people flying in from all over the country, and in true Australian style, it is hardly a sober affair. It was hard to imagine that the races had to be cancelled a few years back when the town and surrounding area was flooded after heavy rain; some rain now would have cooled things down a bit.

We rested for a day and I took the opportunity to check over Matilda and phone the police to let them know we would be tackling the track and that I would be in contact again once we were at Marree. This is also recommended practice.

Before heading for Australia, I had given much thought to how we might communicate with the outside world if we got caught in an emergency situation. Satellite telephones are very expensive, but could be hired, and EPIRBs (Emergency Position Indicating Radio Beacon) are commonly carried in the Outback. I decided on a SPOT Connect unit. This little gadget, about the size of a mobile telephone, works through GPS technology and can be programmed to identify where you are to third parties, to send out pre-programmed emails, and has an SOS button that signals to the emergency services that you need assistance. Fortunately, we never had to use it, but it was insurance, and had we suffered a serious problem it was comforting to know the cavalry would be coming to rescue us.

The Birdsville Track came into being in the nineteenth century when cattle stations in south-west Queensland were seeking a shorter route for droving their animals to the ports of South Australia, then to the railheads at Port Augusta and later Marree. The track is no longer used for this purpose and has become something of a tourist route (for those with suitable vehicles). However, it continues to pass through very remote territory and official websites describe the area as extremely barren, dry and isolated.

The Birdsville Track first became known around the world when Shell, the oil company, made a film about a character known as the Birdsville Postman. Tom Kruse was the local postman based at Marree, at the southern end of the track, and once a fortnight would embark on a challenging journey by lorry to deliver post and other essentials to the remote stations and little communities along the Birdsville Track in those days.

Kruse had all manner of problems to deal with – the sand, dust, heat, flooding, mechanical issues and more but, supposedly, always made it through and was a lifeline to civilisation for the brave souls who tried to scratch a living in the challenging environment. The film, *The Back of Beyond*, was shown around the world and I suspect I saw it in my youth on television. For certain, I have known about the track for as many years as I can remember, so the film must have had quite an impact on me.

Birdsville Track and into South Australia – on our own

I was really looking forward to the journey as completing the 500 km (320 mile) track was another of my bucket list items and was a key element of what I wanted from our adventure in Australia.

We left the campsite in Birdsville early in the morning, and as we drove out of town I knew Pam was feeling very nervous and probably wished she had never agreed to be on the trip.

The tarmac soon ran out leaving the next 500 km to be run on the gravel highway. We passed a couple of road signs providing advice on track conditions and warnings of the remoteness of the wilderness we were about to enter, so I took a photo, a deep breath and headed out into the Strzelecki Desert.

Within a few miles, we passed the entrance to Pandie Pandie Station on our right and could see the homestead buildings surrounded by trees; we were already in South Australia. There would be nothing now for a long, long way. The track was fairly smooth and we were able to bowl along at 80-100 kph (50-60 mph) without any trouble, but it was still very warm. We had agreed to stop for a few minutes every hour or so, and in no time at all Pam was telling me we should take a breather.

The scenery was almost featureless; initially, we were running parallel to low sand dunes on either side of the road, but there were no trees and very little growth other than saltbush. From time to time, we saw kites and crows alongside the road, usually feasting on roadkill, and sadly we added to their feasting by hitting a couple of lizards sitting in the middle of the road that we couldn't avoid. The sound of their bodies hitting the underside of Matilda was none too pleasant, however such incidents are to be expected if one travels the Outback and they are part and parcel of the experience.

Several kilometres to our right as we headed almost directly south was the Diamantina River and the Goyder Lagoon, although both were probably dry as there had been no rain in the region for a long time. This was to our advantage as it meant the track was likely to be in good condition. At about 100 km (80 miles), the track gradually veered round to the west and as we headed on we looked out for a very minor track that would head off east towards Innamincka, but it was so minor we never saw it.

Just occasionally, we could see some cattle in the middle distance, and once we saw a dog sitting in the middle of the road. As we approached, it took off to our right and, whilst we thought it was a dingo, it was black or dark brown in colour. It ran away so quickly, it may have been a wild dog, or just possibly a dog from Alton Downs Station about 20 km (12 miles) to the west and sited on what is known as the Inside (Birdsville) Track.

Resting on the remote 500 km Birdsville Track

The road turned south again. We were now in the Sturt Stony Desert. We came upon the entrance to the Warburton Track which headed off to the north-west and the Simpson Desert. The very tatty and wind-worn sign gave stark warnings of entering the track unprepared. The Birdsville Track remained fairly smooth with occasional rough patches and cattle grids, but nothing that Matilda couldn't cope with easily.

The only respite on the journey to Marree is the Mungerannie Roadhouse which we reached during the afternoon, but not without a scare. The last 50 km (31 miles) seemed to take forever to pass and as we got to about 10 km (6 miles) from the roadhouse, poor old Matilda started crying "Enough!" and spluttered to a stop.

OOO-errrrr!

I had been using petrol until a few miles before this unscheduled stop and had changed to LPG without stopping, just as we had done many times before. I turned over the starter, quietly praying to myself, but she wouldn't fire up. So I switched back to petrol and, after a couple of coughs, the engine started again and we continued as if nothing was wrong – I wasn't going to admit to Pam that I was a little concerned. I had begun to think about what we would do if we couldn't get Matilda going, but after all the warnings I wasn't going to walk off to the roadhouse for help. We would have stayed where we were until someone came along. The problem was, we had seen absolutely nobody on the way down from Birdsville, so may have had to wait for a day or two!

Within minutes, we turned into the short track leading to the Mungerannie Roadhouse and, as we pulled up in front of the hotel, I breathed a sigh of relief!

I also turned to Pam and said, "You have to be brave to travel with Vic!"

"Tell me about it," she replied, wishing, I think, she was sitting beside a hotel swimming pool somewhere more normal.

The hotel was a spread out collection of single-storey buildings including cabin accommodation, the roadhouse itself, a workshop and an odd collection of sheds.

Alongside all this, in front of the hotel, was an open patch of ground that was the campsite area with some rusted hulks of Chevrolet trucks and a bus stop. Yes, a bus stop for the number 37a of Adelaide Metro with a reminder to hail the bus when it came. I don't suppose a bus has ever been this far from Adelaide!

As we were now in South Australia, we had to put our clocks on half an hour. Adjusting our clocks was something we had to do several times as we meandered our way around Australia.

There was no sign of life as we pulled up at the petrol pumps in front of the hotel, but a couple of beeps on the horn led to a bearded guy appearing and he introduced himself as Phil. We went into the bar, the usual collection of eclectic memorabilia adorning the walls and ceiling, and enjoyed a couple of beers. Although we were probably going to be the only people stopping overnight, Phil agreed to cook us a meal later on.

We parked up Matilda; there was no shortage of space to choose from, but we decided against parking too close to the bushes that encircled the site (in case of slithery things); and took a walk round. There was a good amenity block so we had a shower and rested until the appointed meal time.

Phil, the manager of the Mungerannie Roadhouse on the Birdsville Track, was a great Outback character

The next couple of hours were a hoot as Phil regaled us with stories of the Outback and the many characters that either live here or have passed through. I mentioned that I came from the Isle of Man and wondered if he had ever heard of the place.

"Of course I have. We had a backpacker here a couple of years ago who worked behind the bar. He was from the Isle of Man. You're sitting under the Three Legs of Man flag he left behind." And sure enough, the red and gold Manx flag was fixed to the ceiling right above my head and I hadn't seen it.

Phil cooked us a meal, which we ate sitting up at the bar while we watched the film about Tom Kruse, now available on DVD. During the meal, there was a scuffling behind the bar under the counter. Phil grabbed a rifle leaning against the back wall and pointed it at the floor under the television, but didn't pull the trigger. "If you hadn't have been here, I would have shot that rat. It's the last one as I have killed six or seven in the last couple of weeks." I didn't have the heart to tell him I used to be an environmental health officer and managed a team of ten food inspectors working in central London. Shooting rats as a pest control solution wouldn't go down well in the UK!

We talked about how he organised his deliveries because the nearest town, Marree, was still 200 km (125 miles) away and it was a long way from there to any major town. Phil told us he normally had a delivery every three weeks, which included food, fuel, tyres and a host of other essentials he needed to run the hotel and to service visitors' needs. However, as the Christmas holiday was approaching, the next delivery would be four weeks off, so he needed an extra large order. This was all a little bit different from our local Sainsbury's supermarket, which has eight to ten deliveries every day from their regional warehouse.

The next morning, after filling up with petrol, we took our leave of Phil and left him to his lonely existence in one of the most remote roadhouses in Australia.

We were now travelling in the Tirari Desert, although the scenery was much the same as before. We headed on south and soon reached Coopers Creek, a river crossing that I fully expected to be a proper watercourse but which was dried out. The creek is one of the major river systems that form part of the Channel Country we had passed through a few days earlier. Down here it is usually dried out, although when in flood travellers on the track can sometimes wait for days for the water to lower sufficiently to risk a crossing. An alternative is a bypass route with a self-operated ferry.

On our drive down from Birdsville, we had seen no traffic going our way, or going north, although along here we came across a road workers' camp and signs of them maintaining the track, but there was nobody about. In such remote areas, road repair crews often work for weeks at a time before moving on to a new stretch of road to repair.

We also passed through the longest fence in the world, the famous Australian Dog Fence, in our case via a cattle grid with the fence itself leading off into the distance on both sides of the road. The Dog Fence, sometimes also called the Dingo Fence, stretches more than 5,600 km (3,500 miles) from the southern Queensland coast through the central areas of the Outback and south to the southern coast in South Australia along the Nullabor Plain. It was originally constructed in the late nineteenth century to protect flocks of sheep being developed by the pastoralists from the damage inflicted by wild dingoes. The original aims of the fence have largely worked, although in recent times damage to the fence from wild camels means that the maintenance crews who patrol the whole length of the fence on a weekly basis have plenty to do.

As we approached journey's end at Marree, we then came upon a couple of stations at Dulkaninna and Clayton which looked like they were active, although nobody was in sight.

Marree

By late morning, we suddenly hit tarmac for the first time in 500 km (320 miles - the distance from London to Carlisle), and as we drove into Marree, we gave each other high fives and started seeing some other people, the first since Birdsville other than Phil.

Marree stands at the southern end of Lake Eyre with the Birdsville Track running in from the north-east and another long desert track, the Oodnadatta, from the north-west. We hoped to tackle the Oodnadatta later in our trip, so for now we headed into town and stopped at the Marree Hotel for refreshment.

Behind the bar was a tall Englishman from Essex. Andy had been in the RAF but was now travelling Australia. We chatted with him about this and that before heading on south along a mixture of tarmac and gravel roads.

We stopped off briefly to take a look at Farina, now a ghost town but previously a thriving farming community growing grain. Sadly, the hoped for grain harvests never reached their full potential and the community declined after years of drought, leaving behind a school, church, general store, cemetery, hotels, blacksmith, and more. The old underground bakehouse has been restored and is used from time to time when a restoration group holds fundraising meetings.

We stopped in Lyndhurst for fuel and watched as two road trains prepared to head up the Strzelecki Track, probably to the Moomba oil and gas fields where there is a substantial community of workers. Named after one of the early Australian explorers, the track was another of those I would have liked to drive, but time constraints meant it was down the list of priorities. The track runs north to the aforementioned Innamincka and there was a sign at the start warning drivers that there were no services for 452 km (282 miles), the equivalent of driving from London to Newcastle!

At the garage, the owner told us of the hardships that can befall the tough guys who drive the road trains, in particular one road train that headed up the Strzelecki Track and the driver had nine punctures amongst the 80+ wheels on his rig. It would have been very hard work changing those wheels in the heat that pervades the region most of the time.

One of the more interesting parts of the Outback!

Further south, we could just see the opencast coal mine near Leigh Creek, where we decided we would stop for the night. Leigh Creek was rebuilt as a modern community with all new buildings as the original community was in the way of the new coal mine. We did a shop but the place had no character, so we headed for the campsite. Once more we had the place to ourselves, but the amenities were locked up. However, we got the pitch for free as nobody turned up to collect any money.

As we were gradually heading south, we noticed it was getting a bit cooler. We had had a week or so with daytime temperatures well over 40C, and even at night it was over 30C, but now it was a little cooler and more pleasant.

In addition, after the arid and sparse environment of the deserts we had crossed, there was a gradual reappearance of vegetation, and it was even quite green in places.

Murder on a quiet afternoon

In the morning, we headed off again passing the Flinders Range of mountains to our left and stopped briefly at Hawker for coffee. By lunchtime, we were in Quorn, and although we wouldn't know it for a few days, some tragic events were about to unfold.

We stopped in the station car park where there was a Visitor Information Centre and the start of the Pichi Pichi tourist railway that runs over the old Ghan railway track to Port Augusta. I had a look round the station and Pam went to the local supermarket for supplies. We met up and walked around town noting many fine old buildings dating from former glory days, but now rather jaded. The whole place, although pleasant, was one where it seemed nothing much happened. How wrong we were!

We drove on and stopped for the night at Melrose, a collection of houses set out around a couple of road junctions but where all the shops and commercial activities had closed down. The redeeming feature was a cricket pitch and changing facilities, and a reasonably good recreation ground, amongst which people like us could stay with our motorhomes or caravans.

It was lovely, quiet and peaceful, and with few people about, except a Swiss couple in a hired motorhome - needless to say, we swapped notes and had a good yarn.

In the morning, we decided we would try and get to somewhere near Adelaide and have a few days' breather by the sea so made headway through Gladstone, Clare, and Gawler, ending up at the seaside resort of Semaphore, near Port Adelaide. We booked into a campsite overlooking the sea.

Listening to the news that night, we couldn't believe our ears. There had been a double murder in Quorn almost as soon as we had driven away. A 19-year-old local man had murdered a 16-year-old young woman who had spurned his advances. As he burned her body in the local cemetery (which we had passed), he had then murdered another girl, a local disabled Aboriginal resident, supposedly because she had witnessed the incident. This all happened shortly after we had driven through the town; it was awful and we could understand how such a terrible calamity would affect a small community.

Later, we learned more. The murderer had actually volunteered to search for the bodies (as, initially, they had been reported missing), but had been arrested during the search. The disabled girl suffered from dwarfism and was well known in the Outback as a camel rider, her father having instituted the Alice Springs Camel Races.

R&R in Semaphore

We pondered these events while we rested in Semaphore and decided what we would do over the next couple of days. We had driven many miles in Matilda over the last couple of weeks and I needed a breather so we booked in for four nights and relaxed. Matilda needed some R&R too, so we gave her a good clean, inside and out, and checked her over. All seemed well but I needed to get the LPG system checked as I didn't want another scare such as we had on the Birdsville Track.

The campsite was close to the beach and we wandered over there for a walk a couple of times, noting a sign warning of snakes that infest the 30 yards or so of sand dunes between the road and sand. Not like home!

Adelaide itself was about 16 km (10 miles) away and we took the bus in and had a wander round the shops. We then spent a few hours in the South Australian Museum, mainly because it was air-conditioned, but it turned out to be very informative and had well laid out presentations. Adelaide is a great city, set out with the central district surrounded by parkland, and then the suburbs. Later we also visited the railway museum in Port Adelaide.

I looked out a garage in Port Adelaide that specialised in LPG powered vehicles and they found the relay that drove the switch between petrol and LPG was malfunctioning. A replacement was quickly fitted.

We were nearing Christmas and the site had several permanent residents, all single men, who had pitches opposite ours. They were all friendly and wanting to know about our trip, but they were also in the process of putting up their decorations and had lots of fairy lights strung out around their caravans and awnings. At night when lit up, they looked surprisingly Christmassy.

Next to us was a Tasmanian couple who were doing the Big Lap in stages as and when their jobs enabled them to get away. They were used to travelling in remote areas in their 4x4 fitted out a bit like a sandwich truck with fold-out sleeping accommodation on the roof. They had even driven across the Simpson Desert.

The RSL had a dinner evening so we joined forces with Larrie and Kathy and had a good cheap meal while watching a lovely sunset over the Gulf of St Vincent.

Australians are very 'clubby', a favourite being RSL Clubs, a bit like the British Legion Clubs in the UK. However, they are often very big premises with various sports facilities such as bowls, swimming, a gym, as well as bars and restaurants with good value meals and drink. Australians are also inveterate gamblers and the RSLs have plenty of gambling opportunities on the horses, dogs and pokies (one-armed bandits). It is the income from gambling that funds the cheap food and drink. Membership can be easily obtained and we used them regularly around Australia.

It was time to move on so now we headed east up into the Adelaide Hills on twisty roads to Birdwood to see the Australian National Motor Museum. I am a self-confessed petrolhead so found it to be very interesting with information of early motoring pioneers who opened up the remote inland areas of Australia we had just been to.

There followed a lengthy trek south across country very reminiscent of Surrey, ending up at a very quiet beachside community at Sellicks Beach, more or less at the southern end of the Gulf of St Vincent, on which Adelaide lies, and the start of the Fleurieu Peninsula. We expected a campsite to stay at, but couldn't find it, so stopped in the car park above the beach and camped there for the night; no one bothered us. Numerous people were driving on the beach below us, so in the morning we too had a drive up and down before heading off across the peninsula to Victor Harbor.

Victor Harbor

This was a pleasant seaside town facing the Southern Ocean, next stop Antarctica. It had nice beaches, the weather wasn't quite as hot as we had encountered in recent weeks, and the campsite had plenty of shade from tall pine trees. We booked in for a few days.

For the first time, we encountered corellas, white parrot-type birds that gather together in flocks and are very, very noisy. They would rest up in the pine trees in the campsite and then suddenly start flying about, gabbling like crazy, until they settled again in another tree. At first, it was a novelty, but after a while they start driving you mad! They are quite common and we would see many more flocks as we ventured around.

Matilda had a little attention too, as being so close to Christmas it was time to put our own decorations up, so we bought some in town and then wound some tinsel round the bull bar and hung some up inside. But it didn't feel like a real Christmas for us - it was still too warm and we were walking round in shorts and a T-shirt.

Victor Harbor also boasts a horse-drawn tramway, something they have in the Isle of Man, so I was interested in taking a look. Renovated, double-decker trams are now drawn by horses across a causeway to Granite Island as a tourist attraction, the last remnants of an extensive service of trams that used to operate around the area for many years starting in the nineteenth century.

While in Victor Harbor, we heard of an amazing coincidence that occurred back in 1802 just off the coast hereabouts. Two ships, the *Investigator* captained by Matthew Flinders and flying the British flag, and *La Geographie*, a French ship commanded by Nicolas Baudain, were sailing along the coast. Both had been sent by their governments to map the unknown coasts of Australia, or Terra Australis as the British called it then, and New Holland as the French knew it. Both ships were just about as far from their home ports as it was possible to be, although *La Geographie* was sailing with another ship, *La Naturaliste*, but was temporarily alone. The *Investigator* hadn't seen another ship in five months.

By chance, they came upon each other a few miles off Victor Harbor, a meeting that has been likened to the Russian and US astronauts chancing upon each other on the other side of Mars. At the time, the French and British were at war and both ships approached each other with a great deal of caution, but contact was made and cordial meetings took place.

Baudain had been sailing west, Flinders east, so they exchanged mapping and other information, and Flinders recommended nearby Kangaroo Island as a source of food as Baudain's crew were riddled with scurvy.

The bay became known as Encounter Bay, and whilst Flinders gave his name to several Australian features, most notably the Flinders Mountain Range, Baudain's name did not last.

Heading back east

We now faced a trek east back towards Sydney so as to be with our family at Christmas. We had a broad route in mind but were prepared to amend it if something took our attention. We headed off in rain, the first for weeks, to Tailem Bend and Bordertown, where they had an enclosure with about a dozen albino kangaroos. I guess at some time the Burgers of the town thought they might be an attraction to bring in tourists, and now they go out of their way to find more albino kangaroos to add to their little colony. As one might expect, they look a bit spooky, all in white, but were nevertheless something of interest.

We now crossed into Victoria and I wanted to head towards the Grampians NP, so we made our way to Nihill where we picked up a brochure in the Visitor Information Centre for the Little Desert Lodge, which looked like an interesting place to visit. Perhaps we misread the brochure, but when we found it the entrance had high wire fences with barbed wire on top; however, as I pulled up, the gates opened automatically. I figured this was an invitation to go in so I drove on and, after a mile or so, arrived at a parking area amongst offices, accommodation and other buildings.

There was nobody around but I eventually found a Warden's Office and went in to find that the lodge was a private wildlife park, but as it was out of season and nobody was staying, we were welcome to have a look round. The warden gave us a map of the area and we spent a couple of hours wandering round paths amongst the brush spotting wildlife. We saw plenty of kangaroos; well, actually, they spotted us first as they lay dozing under bushes. They would sit up and watch us carefully and usually we could walk to within about ten feet before they would hop away and disappear into undergrowth. Many were carrying joeys, often quite big ones, and we could see their feet sticking out of their mother's pouches. We also saw emu in the woodland, but sadly no malleefowl, a threatened bird species they are breeding at the lodge.

We stopped in Horsham overnight alongside the Wimmera River and took a walk in the evening to a collection of war memorials to the fallen of various wars in which Australians have lost their lives. They were moving reminders that even in this remote town, people fought in wars in far off Europe. Closer to the campsite, Pam found the tennis club and couldn't believe that they had 24 grass tennis courts – even in this small regional town. No wonder Australians are so good at the game!

In our travels over previous weeks, we had seen that Australia is a very flat country, but one of the hilly areas is in the Grampians NP which we visited next, an ancient rocky outcrop that offered great views and splendid waterfalls. We stayed in Halls Creek, a busy tourist town, and drove around the various view spots and clambered down to the waterfalls.

After spending so long in very flat countryside, it was a nice change to see hills and valleys. We drove up to Boroka Lookout which had splendid views over Lake Wartook, as well as another lookout at the Balconies where the view to the north overlooks the heavily forested Victoria Valley. Finally, we ventured to MacKenzie Falls where some tricky steps took us down the side of the falls to a platform at the bottom so we could see the vertical face of rock. It was a great sight and well worth the effort. We were tempted to work our way under the fall of water to cool off, but the rocks were quite slippery, so we erred on the side of caution.

There is quite a bit of Aboriginal art around the park so we headed off down gravel tracks to see some, very faded, coloured rock paintings that were pretty indistinguishable from their surroundings. A pity really, but they were probably tens of thousands of years old and there is a reluctance on the part of the authorities to repaint them. As we found with other rock art we visited, the risk of modern graffiti and 'embellishments' means they must be protected by iron railings and fencing.

The park was subject to a huge bush fire in 2006 which destroyed about 50% of the area; however, it seemed that it has regenerated very well.

Bendigo

Bendigo was our next port of call, and as we drove into town along a tree-lined avenue, the Sacred Heart Cathedral stood tall in front of us, one of the largest churches in Australia. With its tree-lined roads, the city reminded us of France. The city also had an old tramway system, also dating from the nineteenth century, which I had to try. Bendigo's trams operated under various guises until 1972 as they criss-crossed the city serving the suburbs, the length of the lines growing along with the population.

After the service closed down, a trust took over, renovating some trams, and now they run a regular service from the city centre to a northern suburb. They reminded me of the Mountain Railway on the Isle of Man that winds its way from Laxey up to the top of the highest point on the island, Snaefell. The electric tram we rode had fine wooden features, old Victorian style lights, and rumbled along stopping at various places for passengers to alight.

They say that Bendigo is built on gold and there was a huge gold rush in the late nineteenth century when the city prospered and developed very rapidly. It is estimated that about 5,000 shafts were dug, many to great depths, but gradually the seams were worked out and the Central Deborah Mine was the last to close for commercial mining.

The Central Deborah Mine is now a tourist attraction, and although Pam isn't too keen on confined spaces, I persuaded her to try out a visit, and we were glad we did. We were equipped with ear defenders, a helmet with torch and a battery pack, and descended 80ft in a rapid lift to the working level. Our guide was a retired engineer and took us round worked-out galleries, showing us various features, eventually leading us to an alcove where he gave us a demonstration of some of the drilling equipment used. We were warned it was very noisy, so it was on with the ear defenders and he started it up. The level of noise was atrocious and it is hardly surprising that most miners were deaf within a few months of starting work at the mine.

Our guide told us that subterranean Bendigo remains a maze of former workings but with the invention of modern technologies and the increasing price of gold, there have been plans to reopen several mines.

Pam had another tennis treat here as there was a junior tournament going on at the local club. She spent a whole day there and was again envious of their facilities with 30 courts in use.

When we were in New Zealand for a few weeks in a hired motorhome, we met a couple from Boort, a town near Bendigo, and had arranged to visit them. Wally and Kathy were glad to have some visitors and our time with them gave us an insight into life in a rural community, well away from the normal tourist routes. Boort was in the middle of an agricultural area, so most employment was linked to that. Wally had been a lorry driver and a regular run was to take 30 tons of potatoes to Queensland. Olive growing was the other main occupation. They showed us around town, and fed and watered us for a couple of hours.

Time was marching on and we only had a few days to get back to meet our family in Sydney. Our son-in-law, Daz, had his brother and sister-in-law staying with him and had arranged for all of us to spend a night in the Hunter Valley, a popular wine growing region two hours north of Sydney.

So from Boort we headed across country to stay in Deniliquin, and before going to the campsite, we headed into town for some bits of shopping and sweated in the heat, about 38C. Being so close to Christmas, there was a huge decorated tree mounted on a small roundabout at a crossroads in the centre of town, and although we were getting used to Christmas in the heat, it still seemed a bit weird.

The BIG4 campsite had a brand new swimming pool, which we had all to ourselves – a lovely treat after a day's driving. For the first time, we came across the infamous widowmaker tree, the Red River Gum. It has a habit of unexpectedly shedding huge branches during periods of drought, sometimes with inevitable results on anyone passing by. There were several of these trees around the campsite with notices, *"WARNING – These trees may drop branches without warning resulting in serious injury or death"*. We would see similar signs as we travelled around Australia.

The campsite at Deniliquin was part of the BIG4 group and we stayed at many of their sites around the country. Generally they were to a good standard with excellent shower blocks, laundry, kitchen and facilities such as swimming pools and jumping pillows for the kids. Actually, as there was nobody around at this site, we had a go on the jumping pillow - great fun!

Other chains of campsites include Discovery and Top Tourist; not quite as good as BIG4 sites, but quite adequate all the same, and a little bit cheaper. We often stayed in local independent town sites, but the standard of these varied a lot.

Pitches varied as well. Generally, we parked on hard ground with a slab of concrete adjoining, over which the awning could be pulled out. Power outlets were much the same as in the UK, as were drinking water taps, but we had to be wary of the occasional water point described as 'bore water' which was alright for washing, but not for drinking. Bore water is untreated and is often contaminated with chemicals and unsavoury microorganisms.

Most of the larger sites had good disposal points for toilet cassette waste, many installed by the CMCA. Grey water disposal was simple; generally, sites were happy for the waste pipe to discharge under a nearby tree.

Matilda races round Mount Panorama

Back to the trip. For us, it was across arable farming country to Young for a night, and then to Bathurst where I couldn't resist a drive round the world-famous Mount Panorama racing circuit which, unlike UK motor racing, uses closed public roads. Driving round it was a little disconcerting to find traffic coming the other way, although it was obvious one was on a race circuit as the road sides were littered with advertising boards, marshal posts and other paraphernalia associated with a race circuit.

Mount Panorama is 6.2 km (4 miles) long and is home to a 12 hour car race and a 1,000 km (625 miles) race, known as The Great

Race and the most important motor race in Australia. Nearby is the National Motor Racing Museum, but we gave it a miss this time as we had visited it on our first trip to Australia.

After my slight indulgence, we now headed for a *Camps 6* site on a recreation ground in the tiny community of Bylong. It was a pleasant drive through rolling countryside before we reached the village. We checked in at the local grocery store before parking up in the recreation ground. A sign on a noticeboard informed us about an annual attraction, the Bylong Mouse Races, but sadly they occurred a few weeks earlier.

It was the most beautiful evening as we set up for the night at the edge of the recreation ground; it was quiet, a gentle wind took the heat out of the air, and the sun was setting over distant hills. We sat out with our beer and wine, and pondered our travels over the last couple of months. We had seen and experienced so much, been to terrific places and met some amazing people. There was, hopefully, more to come.

Back into Sydney

The next day, we drove over a mountain road through Goulburn River NP and the Great Dividing Range, nearly catching a kangaroo in our bull bar, and it wasn't long before we were in the Hunter Valley and visiting a winery before meeting up with our family. Jenny, our daughter, now had a large baby bump and we had a great family night in a rented bungalow and slept in a proper bed for the first time in ages. In the morning, Christmas Eve, we all headed down to Sydney and were in Manly by lunchtime. After driving along quiet country roads and down deserted rural tracks, we found the madcap driving of Sydney a bit disconcerting, but managed to arrive in one piece and even managed to park Matilda, not a small vehicle by any means, right outside our daughter's place.

We would now spend Christmas and New Year in Manly and leave again early in the New Year. Christmas Day was spent in our daughter's rented cottage right alongside Manly Harbour where we had a traditional Christmas dinner, under the awning as it was raining. We were going to have a swim but the rain put us off, so we left that until New Year's Day when the sun shone. During the break, we went to the Sydney Opera House to see a cabaret, and also went to see the start of the Sydney – Hobart Yacht Race from a friend's house that overlooks North Head and the opening of Sydney Harbour into the Tasman Sea.

Daz's company owned a part share in a motor cruiser, so he took the four of us out for a day all around Sydney Harbour and up a few creeks. We had lunch in a sheltered spot down one creek before returning to the busy main waterway and motored past the Opera House and under Sydney Harbour Bridge. A great day.

On New Year's Eve, there was a party at our daughter's house and we had ringside seats to watch the local New Year firework display in Manly Harbour. Later, we could just see some of the main Sydney firework display over the hill.

It was a lovely break and we could have stayed much longer, but it was time to move on and continue our adventure.

Part 4

* Off to the south
* Canberra
* A look at deep space
* Melbourne
* Great Ocean Road
* Ballarat
* Anyone for golf?
* Into the forests
* Mallacoota
* Attention from the police
* Sampling Australia's health service

West
Wyalong

Balranald   Hay

Narrandera

Wagga
Wagga

Deniliquin   Finley   NSW

Corowa   Albury
Cobram

Echuca   Wangaratta

Shepparton

Bendigo   Benalla

Stawell   Seymour   On

Ararat   VIC   Dargo

Ballarat   Sunbury   B

Cressy   Werribee   MELBOURNE   Maffra
Geelong   Dandenong

Terang   Camperdown   Warragul   Sale
Torquay   Traralgon

Port   Lorne
Campbell   Apollo Bay   Wilsons
          Promontory

BASS STRAIT

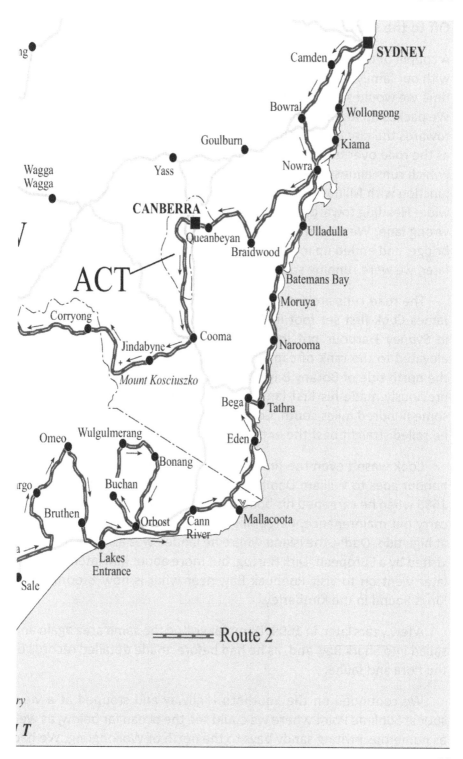

ng

Camden   **SYDNEY**

Bowral   Wollongong

Goulburn   Kiama

Wagga
Wagga   Yass   Nowra

CANBERRA   Ulladulla

Queanbeyan   Braidwood

ACT   Batemans Bay

Moruya

Corryong   Cooma   Narooma

Jindabyne

Mount Kosciuszko

Bega   Tathra

Omeo   Wulgulmerang   Eden

Bonang

rgo   Buchan

Bruthen   Orbost   Cann   Mallacoota
River

a

Lakes
Entrance

Sale

═════ Route 2

Off to the south

A couple of days into the New Year, it was time for a tearful goodbye with our family. We were leaving our pregnant daughter, and the next time we would see her, a new baby would probably have been born. We packed up Matilda and soon we were heading along Military Road towards the city centre. The junction at North Sydney is a nightmare as the road over the Harbour Bridge and through the Harbour Tunnel (which runs almost directly under the bridge) run uphill towards the junction with Military Road, and with various slip roads, it is 14 lanes wide! Heading towards the city centre (CBD), it is easy to get into the wrong lane. We weren't fussed about using either the tunnel or the bridge, and ended up in the lane for the tunnel, and a few kilometres later, we were running south past the airport and out of the city.

The road runs around the edge of Botany Bay where Lieutenant James Cook first set foot in Australia. Most people think he landed in Sydney Harbour but in reality Lieutenant Cook (he wasn't yet elevated to the rank of captain) landed on the Kurnell Peninsula on the north side of Botany Bay. This was on 29ᵗʰ April 1770 and he had previously made his first landfall a few days earlier at Brush Island, some hundred miles south. Cook never saw Sydney Harbour because he sailed straight past the entrance.

Cook wasn't even the first British explorer to visit Australia. That honour goes to William Dampier who landed in Western Australia in 1688 when he careened his boat, the *Cygnet*, on Dirk Hartog Island to carry out maintenance. Careening is the practice of beaching a boat at high tide. Oddly, the island where he landed was also the first to be visited by a European, Dirk Hartog, but more about him later. Dampier later went on to visit Roebuck Bay, near what is now Broome, and Kings Sound in the Kimberley.

A few years later, in 1699, Dampier visited the same area again and sailed into Shark Bay, and, as he had before, made detailed records of the flora and fauna.

We continued on the Southern Highway and stopped at a view spot at Sublime Point where we could see the ocean far below, as well as numerous inviting sandy bays to the north of Wollongong. We had

Part 4

coffee in the cafe, but rather than drop down to the beaches, decided to head inland towards Picton and then south on another main road, the South Western Highway, towards Mittagong and Bowral. We had been recommended to visit Bowral but whilst there were historic buildings, all the shops seemed to be touristy craft shops which we don't much like, so we headed on.

The plan was to make our way back towards the coast, and the road twisted and turned, dropped down a steep escarpment to Kangaroo Valley (although we didn't see any of the iconic Australian marsupial) and then to Nowra. We then headed inland to take a rural route that would lead us to Canberra. We expected the road (with the strange name of Turpentine Road) to be gravel but it had recently been updated to sweeping stretches of tarmac. We started looking for a stopover for the night but whilst the first potential spot at Sassafras had impressive rock outcrops, we couldn't find anywhere suitable to pull in. We also stopped at nearby Tianjara Waterfalls, but stopovers were forbidden in the car park. We did, however, take a walk to the falls but the very dry spell meant that the impressive falls were virtually dry with only a slight trickle of water dropping to the valley floor.

Once again, the semi drought conditions were in the news which was full of reports of serious bush fires, especially in Victoria where several people had died. As we were now in a national park, we had seen signs banning open fires because of the risks, but we were also aware of thunder and lightning that was now filling the greying skies.

The tarmac ended at the small community of Narriga and we continued looking out for a place to set up camp for the night. We found a turning with a signpost to Wog Wog Campsite, and, about 5 km (3 miles) down the track, turned off into a parking area with a pit toilet and some noticeboards with information about the area. The surrounds of the camp area were heavily wooded and there were no obvious walking tracks so we only wandered around within sight of Matilda. It was easy to see how going further afield could get us lost and we might have been wandering around for hours, as seems to happen all too often in this part of the world.

91

We settled down for the night amidst continuing thunder and lightning, but little or no rain. No vehicles passed us on the track until about 2.00 a.m., when I awoke to a blue flashing light as a couple of emergency vehicles drove by, we guess looking for possible lightning strikes that could start a fire.

In the morning, we headed back to the main track and drove on to Braidwood and joined the main highway towards Canberra. Along here we came upon a *Camps 6* site that was very busy and highlighted the variation in camping possibilities around Australia. Wog Wog had been isolated and remote and we were the only people there. This parking area near a river bridge along the road between Braidwood and Queanbeyan was clearly very popular and even at about 11.00 a.m., when we passed by, there were at least 20 caravans and motorhomes parked up amongst some bushes and trees.

We stopped in Queanbeyan for a walk round and timed a visit to the Visitor Information Centre just right as they were about to close for the day. It was a Sunday and the town was very quiet, but it was becoming very hot again with the temperature in the high thirties and we sought shade wherever possible as we wandered round.

Canberra

It was only a short drive on to Canberra, the capital city of Australia, where we planned to stay for several days. We checked into Canberra South Motor Park at Fyshwick on the main road into town and were soon chatting with various neighbours, all Australians. The temperature was still high and one of our new friends said he was taking his family to the various indoor attractions in the city as they were all air-conditioned and mostly free. It sounded like a good idea to us.

Canberra was one of the first purpose-built capital cities in the world. It was constructed on land in south-east NSW, land that would become the Australian Capital Territory (ACT). Starting from scratch, it was possible to lay out a city with wide avenues and shopping hubs in each of the residential neighbourhoods. There was ample parking, even for Matilda, at all the key attractions, and lovely shaded parks to walk in. In the centre was a huge body of water, Lake Burley Griffin, named after the American architect who won the competition to design the city.

Nearby were the major national institutions, and first we visited the Royal Australian Mint where the viewing galleries of the actual presses stamping out coins had displays of banknotes and coinage. The guide was a hoot and told us the story of the Australian Olympic swimming team. There were great expectations of the team at the London Olympics in 2012 but they had returned home with hardly any medals. Supposedly, they had been invited to visit the Mint so they could all be shown what gold looked like!

After lunch, we headed for the Australian Parliament building which has been built into a hill and part of the roof is turfed. We were able to park Matilda in an underground car park for free and to wander round much of the building unheeded. We also took a guided tour, and whereas Westminster is cramped, ornate and full of history, this building was spacious and stylishly modern. We saw both chambers, which follow the Westminster pattern, and learned that the office for the Senators (equivalent of the Lords) has a coin-operated machine for fried chips!

The next day, we started out with the High Court of Australia, the highest court in the nation but sited in a rather brutal, modern building in the administrative area. The court was in recess so there were no hearings and the building was very quiet with just a few visitors. The guides, two in particular, were very entertaining, both being former senior police officers with an abundance of stories. One was about the kangaroo and emu that are part of the Australian coat of arms – supposedly chosen because they are the only creatures on Earth that cannot walk backwards; Australia is a nation moving forward, we were told.

Next, it was over the road to the National Portrait Gallery where the star feature was a portrait of HM Queen Elizabeth II painted as part of her Diamond Jubilee. Round the corner was the National Gallery with samples of many Australian artists as well as Picassos and Monets, but we didn't stay long as we are not great fans of the arts.

Finally, we ended the day at the National Library where there was an absorbing display depicting the history of the continent since European colonisation. Many of Lt. James Cook's documents, memorabilia, and other special and rare documents and artefacts were available for viewing, and I was fascinated.

Most people, if asked "Who discovered Australia?", will answer "Captain Cook". It was at the National Library that we first found out this was far from the case. If we ignore the indigenous population who have inhabited Australia for as long as 50-60,000 years, the first European visits to the continent were long before Cook happened upon Botany Bay on his way back from recording an eclipse of the sun in Tahiti.

The first recorded visit to what we now know as Australia was made by Dirk Hartog, a Dutchman who captained the *Eendracht*, a vessel of the Dutch East India Company who happened upon an island off western Australia while en route to Batavia (Jakarta) in Indonesia. He landed on the island, which now bears his name, and left behind a pewter plate to mark his visit. This was on 25th October 1616, over 150 years before Cook. Because Hartog was a trader, he took no interest in claiming the land for his country, and, after his landing, headed off for his intended destination.

It was Cook who became the first person to visit the eastern coast of Australia and later claim the eastern seaboard as British territory.

On our third day in Canberra, we went to the National War Memorial and had a guided tour lasting 90 minutes that took us through the commemorative plaques for those lost in various conflicts in which Australia has been involved (61,000 of the military). The tour also took us to the tomb of the Unknown Soldier, and also an extensive war museum with dramatic and informative displays. Parts of the museum were very moving and we ended up spending the whole day there, and could easily have spent more time there had we not got another agenda and needed to move on.

For our last day in Canberra, we took ourselves to the National Museum of Australia and spent the day looking at the numerous galleries and displays. I was particularly taken with a small display dedicated to Joan Richmond who, in the '30s, had driven her car from Melbourne to Palermo, Sicily in order to start from there and take part in the Monte Carlo Rally. She then stayed in Europe for a few years competing in more rallies and races, even winning a 1,000 mile race at Brooklands, which is just down the road from where we live, before returning to Australia and vanishing into relative obscurity.

We were also moved by an account of a fellow Quayle, Simon Quayle, who survived the Bali bombing in 2002 that killed over 200 people including 88 Australians. He was coach to the Kingsley Amateur Football Club, a club from Perth, who went to Bali as an end of season celebration. They were having a good time in the Sari Club when the terrorist blast took place and seven of the team were fatally wounded. A terrible tragedy.

A look at deep space

It was time to leave Canberra and our first port of call was hidden away in the Canberra Hills – Canberra Deep Space Communications Complex (CDSC), used by NASA to track space flights including long-distance satellites heading out to Mars, Jupiter and beyond. There was a small museum and some moon rock, and we learned that CDSC received the first message delivered from the moon by Neil Armstrong – *"One small step for man, one giant leap for mankind"* before passing the memorable words on to Houston and the rest of the world.

Our plan was to head south through Tharwa, a tiny hamlet with an amazing old fashioned shop and petrol station, and into Namadgi National Park. However, at the Visitor Information Centre, we learned that whilst we could drive through on the main route, the fire risks had closed all the campsites and many of the side roads. So we went on, much of the trip on gravel roads, before ending up in Cooma, where we stopped for the night. The campsite also had ski equipment for hire as we were now at the edge of the winter ski area – the temperature was 37C!

In the morning, we headed west and stopped briefly beside Lake Jindabyne where the town of the same name was rebuilt on high land at the southern end of the new lake. It was created to form a reservoir as part of the Snowy River scheme. Unfortunately, the new town seemed to have little character and was somewhat soulless.

We weren't too sure what to expect of the Australian Alps but they turned out to be very picturesque. We headed for Thredbo, which is one of several ski resorts around the area, from where we took the tortuous mountain road over Dead Horse Gap and past Mt Kosciuszko to Currying. The road is a toll road, but you can go through for free if you don't stop, other than for fuel in the village.

For 80 km (50 miles), it was up and down hills, with bend after bend, through dense forest with fine views. These are the highest mountains in Australia, and in winter the area is deep with snow – we could see some on the south-facing slopes.

We rounded one corner and a kangaroo sitting on the verge nearly breathed his last and became lunch as he hopped across the road in front of Matilda. We also nearly ran over a blue-tongued lizard. We stopped at Wodonga for the night and the next day zipped 300 km (190 miles) down the motorway into Melbourne and found the nearest campsite to the city centre at Braybrook in the western suburbs.

Melbourne

All the talk was of the weather; even Australians had had enough of the heatwave which had not eased a bit. With many national parks closed due to the fires, the campsite was packed as people had to change their plans. Birdsville, which we visited a couple of months ago, had recorded 48C the day before, as had White Cliffs, an opal mining town we stayed at on our first visit to Australia in 2009. In the same region, 50C+ was being recorded and the weathermen had to rethink their weather charts and add another colour for temperatures ranging up to 54C!

We had a good reason to visit Melbourne; Pam, the tennis fan, would be visiting the Australian Open tennis tournament, spending three whole days watching the earlier rounds. We don't live too far from Wimbledon, and in my youth I sometimes delivered the newspapers to the All England Lawn Tennis and Croquet Club, as the site is officially known, and we have both been regular visitors. In recent years when she has not been successful in the ballot, Pam has queued, often for many hours, to get in and then often struggled to get a decent spot to view the tennis.

In Melbourne, the experience was wholly different. On the first day, she got a bus into the city centre from outside the campsite, then a free tram to the courts complex, and had to queue for only a few minutes to obtain a three-day pass. Then it was a short wait for the complex to open and she was then able to get an all-day courtside seat on the Margaret Court Arena at no extra cost, usually in front row seats. She was very satisfied.

Meanwhile, I toured some of the sights of the city, including rides on another ancient tramway system, a visit to the Old Gaol, Police Museum, Immigration Museum and a re-enactment of the trial of Ned Kelly, the infamous Australian bushranger (outlaw).

I also sought out another garage. The LPG system still wasn't working properly and I needed to get it fully functional before heading off again into more of the remoter areas of Australia. I eventually found a specialist company and they identified a faulty dashboard switch and replaced it. For evermore it worked fine and once again Sydney RV Centre covered the cost under the warranty.

Great Ocean Road

Next on our agenda was to visit a former work colleague of Pam's, Regina, who lives south of Melbourne at the lovely seaside and surfing resort of Torquay. Regina and her family have a lovely house a couple of hundred yards from Torquay's famous beach, one of the best in Australia. They showed us round the town and we stayed the night in their guest bungalow.

In the morning, we visited a farmers' market on the front and also took a look at nearby Bells Beach, a famous surfing location which is why Torquay is said to be the surfing capital of Australia.

After saying cheerio to our friends, we headed out once more towards the Great Ocean Road, a well-known coastal road that runs along, or close, to the sea. The road is one of the great ocean drives, and, for most of its route, hugs the coast and sweeps around small coves or behind wide, open bays. We took our time and stopped regularly, staying at a couple of campsites which were very busy because it was still the school holidays.

We took two side roads off the Great Ocean Road, the first a well-known location for koala spotting. We drove slowly up the designated road through a forest, and, after a while, spotted several koalas curled up and nestling in branches just off the road. A special treat was to see a young koala, which at first was hugging its mum five metres (18 feet) up a tree, and then separated itself and climbed higher up. There were also some kangaroos shuffling about in the brush, but they were hard to spot because of their camouflaged coat.

Not far away, we stopped on another side road alongside a golf course to see about a dozen grey kangaroos grazing alongside golfers as they lined up for their final shots to the green, a hazard I am not used to when I play.

The first campsite was the most expensive we stayed in during the whole trip. To be fair, it was school holiday time, it was adjoining a pleasant beach, had an attractive river running through the middle of the site, but it was A$72 (about £45!) for the night, with no power.

We took a side turning on a road that led to the coast and Cape Otway, where the oldest surviving lighthouse in Australia looks out over the eastern end of the Bass Straight. The lighthouse was constructed in 1848 and has continued to be in use ever since.

Cape Otway was often the first sight of land that ships from Europe would see as they crossed the South Australian Bight and, unfortunately, many were shipwrecked on the cliffs in the area – thus the lighthouse was built. We took a climb to the top and a walk round the surrounding area, and on the way back to the main road, we saw more koalas asleep in the trees right over the busy road.

Koalas spend most of their day sleeping, and this one, seen in a tree over the road leading to Cape Otway, VIC, was no exception

The Great Ocean Road is perhaps the largest war memorial in the world as it was built in memory of the tens of thousands of Australian soldiers who were killed in World War I. Returning soldiers, many of whom were unemployed as it was the Depression, were given the construction work as and when money was available and the 350 km (220 miles) route linked up some very remote communities and in time would draw in many tourists to the area.

A particular attraction were the Twelve Apostles, limestone outcrops that can be seen from various viewing spots. The main Visitor Information Centre was crawling with Japanese and Chinese tourists, but it was still possible to find spots where the scene was dramatic and less crowded.

Surprisingly, it was here that I saw an echidna, a hedgehog-type mammal that is fairly common in Australia. A small crowd of tourists were leaning over the rails of one of the broad walks leading to a view spot, and low and behold there was the echidna scratching around in the dirt for insects. However, it soon disappeared under the walk and wasn't seen again.

The second campsite we stopped at was at Port Campbell, a small seaside resort which was nice and quiet, in contrast to the hustle and bustle further along the main road near the Twelve Apostles.

Ballarat

We planned to head east pretty soon so as to be reasonably close to Sydney, should our granddaughter (we knew it would be a girl) make an early appearance, so we took roads north to Ballarat and stayed the weekend. The city has many large, imposing buildings, the result of wealth created by gold mining in the nineteenth century. They even had a gold museum which we visited and heard how popular metal detecting has become in recent years. Hardly surprising when someone had just found a nugget worth about A$300,000!

On a trip such as ours, a lot of reading goes on, and both of us had recently read *The Life of Pi* by Yann Martel, and we noticed it was showing in the cinema in the middle of town. It was very hot, the cinema had air conditioning so it was a no-brainer to go in. Apart from a surreal episode on a supposed island, the film seemed to be a good representation of the book. We certainly enjoyed the break from the heat outside.

Lake Wendouree on the west of the city was used as the rowing and canoe venue for the 1956 Melbourne Olympics, and we took a very pleasant 6 km walk around the lake on a sunny afternoon in the company of many families enjoying the Australia Day Bank Holiday.

Ballarat had suffered a mini tornado a few months previously, which caused a lot of damage. We visited a caravan dealer and they had a display of about 25 caravans, most of which had been damaged in the storm. Whilst some had been repaired, the sides of many were still peppered with dents from the hailstones. On another occasion, we saw a Subaru estate car with similar damage and were warned to take heed of weather warnings when hailstones are expected. The advice is to get the vehicle under cover, or at least covered with some protective sheeting.

Anyone for golf?

The next day was a transit day and we headed east back through Melbourne and onward along the Princes Highway towards Warragul and Traragon. We were looking for a campsite from our *Camps 6* directory and it listed a site at Maffra Golf Club about 30 km (20 miles) away so we thought we would give it a try. Sure enough, there were half a dozen powered pitches adjacent to the first tee and we had full access to the club house and facilities, all for A$10. After finishing our meal, we headed for the bar and had a few drinks with a couple of local teams playing pool.

I am a golfer so I asked about the possibility of getting a round in. "No problem," said the steward. "I can find you some clubs to use if you want, but you will need to be careful."

"Why's that?"

"There are a lot of snakes about at present, especially in the rough."

"Oh, that's a pity. The way I play, I tend to see a lot of rough. I think I'll pass." So I gave it a miss.

Into the forests

But the next day made up for it. I am a 4x4 enthusiast - that was one reason for taking the opportunity to buy Matilda - and I knew the area to the north, the Victoria Highlands, were very popular for off-roading through the extensive forests. I thought we should take a look and maybe give it a try and see what Matilda was really capable of.

First, we checked there was no risk from forest fires and then headed for Dargo and had some lunch in the pub there. We chatted with a couple who had just driven through the forest from Omeo, about 80 km (50 miles) away, but other than some rain and mist and the track being a bit cut up, they had found the track alright in their Mitsubishi Shogun. The landlord gave us a tip as to where the route was a bit unclear, so off we went.

We soon turned off the tarmac and the light rain started together with low mist, but for me there was the red mist!

It was great 4x4 driving – up, down, some rough sections but mainly smooth, but, because of the mist, no views. As expected, the route was unclear at some places, with many junctions unsigned, but we seemed to head the right way, and after a couple of hours, and a few short stops, hit the tarmac again on the run into Omeo. Of course, we could have got lost, had a puncture or breakdown, but the beauty of driving Matilda was we were self-reliant and could easily have stopped overnight in the forest if necessary.

As usual, on gravel roads, I had let the tyres down to about 30 psi, and rather than use the air compressor to inflate them again, headed into a garage in Omeo. We stopped at the first one we came to, because for all we knew, it was the only one in town, filled up with petrol and went to use the air line. It wasn't working and despite protests from me, the owner told us she was packing up for the day and wouldn't put it on again. Tough!

I pulled along the road to get my own air compressor out and found there was another garage just round the corner where the owner was also just packing up for the day. However, his attitude was one of helpfulness; yes use my air line, no problems, no I don't want anything for it, where are you from - an entirely different experience!

We stopped in the campsite down by the river and the lady running the site tried to get us to take a guinea pig away with us; she had been breeding them and had too many. Somehow we resisted the offer, but did chat about the local area and places we hoped to visit in the next few days.

The road through Omeo is the Great Alpine Road, and to the north-west it was closed because of the persistent forest fires that would eventually take some lives near Bright, not far way. Fortunately, we would be heading the other way.

Driving back south towards the coast again, we pulled off the road to stop for lunch, crossing a little bridge to park up in a sunny glade away from the road. All was still and peaceful but we could hear a strange pinging, bell-like noise, one we could not identify. It sounded slightly metallic, and whilst we thought it might be some seed pods popping, or an animal call, we just couldn't place it. It would be a day or two before we had an answer.

Lakes Entrance was a good stopover for a couple of days. It was a busy little town with great fish restaurants and Pam, who had been knitting a blanket for the baby, even got some excellent advice and some personal tuition on crocheting the edging from the local haberdashery shop.

I had enjoyed the forest driving so thought I would try some more and picked up some good routes that were suitable for Matilda at the Visitor Information Centre. We headed out to Orbost and then went north through more forest tracks for a couple of hours. Once or twice, we had to stop and clear fallen tree debris from the track and wished we had a saw with us. We also saw several wild boar carcases, a couple of which were lying in the middle of the road. The carcases were bloated and had clearly been dead for many days but we never found out why they were there.

Australia isn't all desert, and the Victoria Highlands made a
pleasant change from the dry, arid regions we were used to

We stopped overnight in the car park at Little River Gorge where there should have been a waterfall, but with so little rain there was just a trickle of water dribbling over the rocks.

We had been warned that the track on to McKillops Bridge was very narrow and hazardous and the road sign made it very clear – *"Steep narrow winding road. Limited passing areas available for next 11 km"*. There was another sign advising caravans not to venture any further.

We headed on, and yes, an average driver might have found it a bit intimidating. It was narrow with big drops, but it was nothing we hadn't encountered in South America. The locals had no problem with it either as one told us she regularly drove her daughters to rounders matches along the road.

We stopped at a camping area near the bridge, a wide wooden structure, quite picturesque, and had a walk round and watched canoeists white water rafting on the river. The trip back to the coast was something else as it was a great driver's road, especially as light rain was making the track a little slippery. The first 50 km (31 miles) were on gravel, but mostly twisty downhill and Matilda was running perfectly. I had FWD engaged and we swung from corner to corner, drifting occasionally and I just enjoyed the driving. There was another outbreak of red mist and it was absolutely brilliant.

We ended up back at Orbost, stocked up on food and headed on to nearby Marlo on the coast where the campsite overlooked extensive beaches that looked very inviting. We stayed a couple of nights and other travellers here were very friendly.

In particular, we met a Rhodesian couple, now living in Australia, with two lovely Rhodesian Ridgeback dogs. They were great company and Bob (not his real name) had been in the Rhodesian equivalent of the SAS and, so he claimed, had once come across Robert Mugabe, then considered to be a terrorist. Bob could have shot him there and then but was ordered to let him live! The world works in mysterious ways.

Mallacoota

Mallacoota was our next port of call, right down in the south-east corner of this amazing continent. As we were having such fun with Matilda, we decided to take a series of off-road tracks along the coast rather than the main road. These turned out to be rougher and more difficult than anything we had tried before, but Matilda was up to the job and coped well; the main problem was avoiding low branches.

Mallacoota was another small town with great beaches and there was a great campsite alongside the lagoon. It was a bit busy but large enough to take the number of caravans, motorhomes and campers present, and the beach was almost empty. The waves were big but we put on our swimmers and enjoyed the refreshing sea.

It was hard to leave Mallacoota; it was one of the best places we stayed at; laid-back, great beach, good food in the restaurants, and friendly, pleasant people. We even met a local lady who had been to the Isle of Man.

The baby date was approaching so we had to hit the road again. We crossed into New South Wales and headed north to Eden, a fishing community. We visited the Eden Killer Whale Museum here, an interesting and informative place dedicated to the orcas that are often seen in local waters.

In the campsite we heard the pinging, bell-like noise again, as we would over the next few days, and found out that it was the call of the bellbird – a bird that is often heard, but rarely seen. In fact, the locals told us it was a bit of a pest as the noise is a bit bothersome after a while.

During the last couple of weeks, the windscreen had developed a small crack and the off-road driving and consequent flexing of Matilda's chassis had caused it to spread across the screen and it needed replacing. Driving into Marimba, we spotted a repair place beside the main road so stopped and got it fixed (at almost no cost as it was covered on the insurance), and as time was marching on, we headed to a campsite at nearby Pambula.

We parked up and found we were surrounded by semi-tame kangaroos that were at home wandering around the campsite. All very nice, but they left their faeces all over the place, so it was a bit messy!

Chatting to our neighbour, a local from Canberra, the subject somehow got around to classic cars. "I know just the place for you to visit," he said, and made a phone call.

The next day, he sent us just down the road to the Sapphire Coast Historic Vehicle Club, a club that has its own premises including a large workshop, clubhouse and car storage barn. A couple of members were doing some maintenance on the clubhouse and offered to give us a private tour of the cars in store. They took the dust covers off all 50 cars and told us about the owners and history of some of the cars. Most of the classics were European cars, their condition being variable – some pristine, others in need of some TLC, but it was a great visit and a nice surprise.

A few miles up the road was Potoroo Palace Native Animal Sanctuary, a small zoo that we thought was worth a visit. To be fair, it was a bit run-down and scrappy, but the staff were very enthusiastic about their charges and keen to teach visitors all about them.

In particular, we learned about the echidna, the hedgehog-type animal I had seen on the Great Ocean Road. We watched one feeding and extend its very long tongue to pick up larvae from a dish. The staff also got a 3½ metre (12 foot) black-headed python out of its cage and let it slither around on the lawn while the visitors, ourselves included, stroked it (a first) and took photos.

The next few days were uneventful as we meandered our way towards Sydney, so we thought it was time to pay a visit to Rick Stein, the well-known chef. He is an Australiaphile and has a restaurant at Mollymook, and whilst we would have loved to partake of a meal there, the visit was on behalf of our daughter, Jenny.

She was considering organising an office outing there and asked if we would pop into the establishment and get some details. We drove into Mollymook, yet another pleasant seaside town with a wide sandy beach, and at the end of the promenade had to get up a steep hill (Matilda wasn't very good on sealed roads that were steep hills; the rear driving wheels tended to lose grip and spin).

We were on narrow roads, but soon found the hotel where the restaurant was based, a boutique-style place, hardly one that would want a dusty old motorhome outside. We managed to find a tight parking spot nearby and wandered in. It was mid-afternoon, so there were no restaurant guests about and the mâitre d' was happy to hand over a sample menu for us to take away. It made interesting reading later on when we had our standard meat and two veg for our evening meal!

Carrying on, we stopped off at Kiama and nearby Shoalhaven. We chanced upon a pub at Jambaroo where we had lunch in the rear function room which had been dedicated to the memory of Johnny Warren, a noted Australian footballer. After a successful career as a player, Johnny had gone on to be a coach, administrator, writer and broadcaster. In recognition of his work in promoting the sport in Australia, Johnny was awarded the FIFA Centennial Order of Merit by Sepp Blatter, the President of FIFA. Johnny was also awarded an MBE and an OAM (the Medal of the Order of Australia). Like so many things on our Australian odyssey, this was a chance find but the memorabilia offered a fascinating and interesting record of a man who was obviously a remarkable guy.

Kiama was a pleasant little fishing port and tourist centre, and had two blowholes, one in the middle of the harbour area which wasn't very active due to the tide times, but the other smaller blowhole, a short walk from our campsite, threw up a 30ft plume of water and was very impressive.

Heading on north, we took a look at Hyams Beach which lies on the southern side of Jervis Bay, and, according to the *Guinness Book of Records*, has the whitest sand on the planet. It was a weekend, and, the resort being very popular, was very busy, but we managed to park Matilda and took a barefoot walk along the beach with our feet squeaking in the fine sand.

Chatting to a local in a nearby cafe, we found that there was a patch of land just over the hill that is the smallest state within Australia. The Jervis Bay Territory is a parcel of land with a couple of villages that is technically an offshoot of the Australian Capital Territory (Canberra). Apparently it was created to provide a seaside leisure resort for the inhabitants of Canberra when it was first built, and although the land is administered from Canberra, for all practical day-to-day purposes it makes no difference.

Attention from the police

Driving north on the main road, Australia's Route 1, we had our only serious interaction with the Australian police. We were travelling along with other traffic and were second in line following a horsebox being towed by a 4x4. There were four or five other cars behind us. As we motored along, I spied a police car parked on the nearside verge, and as we were well within the speed limit, paid no heed. We all passed by, and it was obvious the copper was checking our speed.

A few minutes later, we could hear a siren and see blue lights behind us and the same police car came speeding up on the offside, passed all the traffic and disappeared into the distance. A couple of miles later, there he was with his speed camera checking us all again, but as he didn't catch anyone, he came and passed us all a second time with his siren and blueys on, and then checked us all yet again further up the road – without success. So be warned.

We heard about an outdoor leisure show at the racecourse near Wollongong so headed there to spend the day and look around. There was a good display of caravans, motorhomes, camping trailers and all the equipment and accessories that go with RV-ing, and I came away with a bundle of leaflets and ideas.

In particular, there was an educational presentation all about the venomous snakes of Australia. On display and being handled by a trained keeper were a taipan, western brown, red belly, death adder, and tiger snake, all nasties in the top ten venomous snakes worldwide. The handler lifted them from sacks with a handling stick and showed them to the gathered throng. He also showed everyone how to apply a snake bite bandage – you never know when you might need one here in Australia. I had a word with the handler and shook his hand; well, part of it because some fingers and part of his palm had been amputated following a nasty snake bite. You live and learn the hard way in Australia!

There was no news of the baby, so as we were now very close to Sydney, we decided to head on into the city. After the quiet roads we had encountered in recent weeks, we found the traffic a bit manic, but were soon through the tunnel and drove on to the campsite at Narrabeen again. We set ourselves up and planned to wait for the baby to arrive, then stay a couple of weeks before setting off for WA and hopefully a drive around the north coast via Darwin and Cairns.

Little Amelia was eventually born at the Mater Hospital in Sydney on 24th February 2013 weighing 8lbs 4oz (3.75kg). Everything was fine, and Mum and Dad, not to mention both grandparents, were very proud. We felt very lucky to be there, as our trip to Australia was planned and booked long before we had any news that our daughter was pregnant.

Sampling Australia's health service

Then something very unexpected happened. We were getting ready to head off again and were shopping in the local mall, and I remember parking Matilda, but not much more for the next 90 minutes. Apparently we went into Woolworths, and while there I mentioned to Pam that I wasn't feeling too good and would go back to the van and wait for her.

She must have felt something was wrong because she came with me, and, for about an hour, kept me company while she decided what to do. She tells me someone asked about Matilda and I couldn't think straight so asked her to speak to the chap; most unusual. Getting worried, Pam did the stroke test – *FAST (FACE – could I smile?; ARMS – could I lift them up?; SPEECH – was my speech slurred?; TIME – time to get help)* - but I seemed fine. However, she felt it would be prudent to take me to the local hospital at Mona Vale, only a couple of miles away.

It was about now that I began to be aware of what was happening. In A&E, an English doctor did various tests and I had a CAT scan. He was thinking that maybe I had had a stroke so arranged for me to be transferred by ambulance to Manly Hospital, which had a specialist stroke ward. Later in the day, I was taken to have an MRI scan at a private facility at Dee Why, but by now, whilst I was feeling a little shocked and fragile, I wasn't too bad. The medics felt differently, and as it was a Friday, I would have to stay in hospital until Monday.

The weekend went slowly. Pam had to go and get Matilda from the hospital car park and drive her back to the campsite, and then get to and from the hospital to visit me.

By Saturday morning, I was feeling 100%, although worried that I may have had a stroke and how that might impact our trip. I felt a bit of a fraud as next to me on the ward were patients who were clearly very ill, whilst I was sitting with Pam on the balcony in glorious sunshine overlooking Sydney Harbour watching a cruise ship and the harbour ferries come and go.

By Monday, I was getting really cheesed off but was pleased when I was discharged. I was advised there was no sign of a stroke and I had probably had a TGA (transient global amnesia), a condition whereby a patient has a sudden blanking out of the mind for a short duration. It was something they knew little about and could find little about in the research papers, except it was unlikely to recur.

But, and it was quite a big 'but', the MRI scan had revealed a growth on my pituitary gland which was something that did need attention, and I was being referred to an endocrinologist at the Royal Sydney Hospital; I'd had no idea of this problem. There was another but – no driving for at least two weeks. We were stuck in Sydney – good news because Pam could see more of the new baby and I could get further medical help, but it was eating into our time in Australia.

We hung around in Sydney waiting for the appointment at the Royal Sydney. Meanwhile, I had another MRI scan and a blood test, and in due course, we got a bus to the hospital. The endocrinologist was a very pleasant young lady of Asian extraction. She told me the growth was significant and needed urgent treatment by way of medication and in our circumstance more detailed attention could wait until we got home to the UK.

The growth would need monitoring by way of blood tests while we were still in Australia, so the doctor gave me a series of request forms that we could take to hospitals as we travelled to get regular blood tests. The results would be forwarded to her and she would contact us if urgent action was needed. She also gave us a covering letter that explained my condition and which I could give to a medic if I felt the need to go to a hospital. I was also cleared to drive again, and after thanking her for her terrific help, we determined to leave in the next few days.

Incidentally, nearly all this treatment was covered by a reciprocal arrangement between the NHS and the Australian health care system. I felt very lucky as Manly Hospital was ten minutes' walk from our daughter's house and I had been taken ill only minutes from another major hospital. So easily it could have occurred in the Outback when I might have had to rely on the Royal Flying Doctor Service and ended up in a remote hospital.

An odd coincidence occurred when I paid my last visit to see the endocrinologist. As I walked in to the consulting room, she introduced us both to Emma, a trainee doctor on an exchange from the UK, who would sit in on the session. We got talking and it turned out she was from Surrey and lived about 16 km (10 miles) from us. She mentioned that her dad, David Russell-Jones, was a consultant at our local hospital and I mentioned I had heard the name but could not place him.

When we returned home, I saw my own GP and had a referral to the local hospital and who did I see? Professor David Russell-Jones! It turned out I had met him before in connection with the Lions Club charity work I am involved with. Small world!

"God bless America. God save the Queen.
God defend New Zealand
and thank Christ for Australia."

Russell Crowe
(Actor)

Part 5

* The Big Lap
* Elvis lives
* The Long Paddock
* Tennis history
* Condo 750
* On again
* Into the Flinders Range
* Feral food
* The Oodnadatta Track
* William Creek
* Pink Roadhouse
* Alice Springs
* West MacDonnell Range
* Uluru
* South on the Stuart Highway
* Nullabor Plain

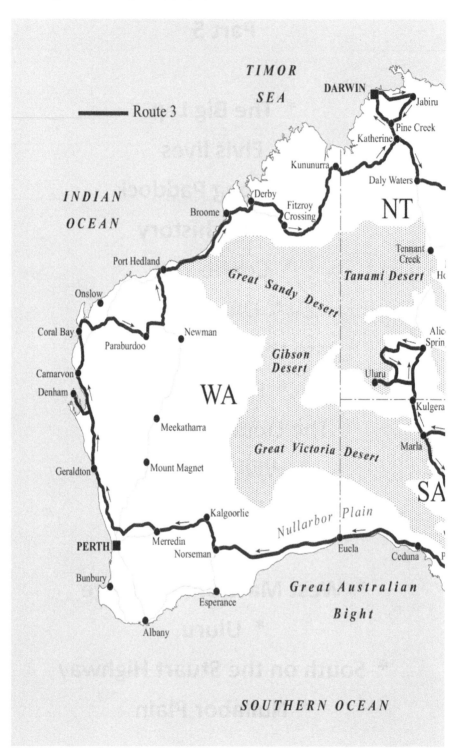

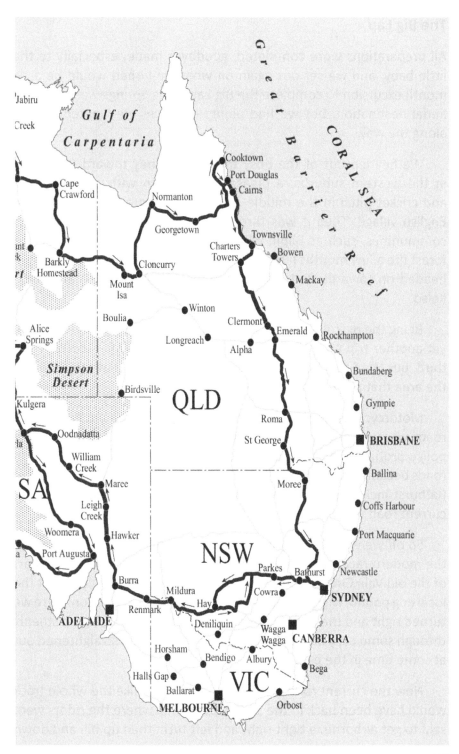

The Big Lap

All preparations were completed, goodbyes made, especially to the little baby, and we set out again on what we hoped would be a six month excursion to complete the Big Lap. Alice Springs was to be our initial destination, but we had plenty of places we wanted to visit along the way.

We headed out of the busy traffic of Sydney toward Richmond in the western suburbs, a pleasant little town with an open park and cricket pitch in the middle of town making it look very like an English village. Then it was through the Blue Mountains and small communities, such as Bilpin which, sadly, would be devastated in a forest fire a few months later. We stopped in Lithgow for a break, then headed on towards Bathurst to stop at a BIG4 campsite at nearby Kelso.

Being the petrolhead that I am, it was inevitable that I would take yet another trip around the famous Mount Panorama racetrack, my third, but I had also heard about motorcycle racing that took place in the area that pre-dated the famous track.

Motorcycle racing on closed (and I suspect not always closed) roads was very popular in the 1930s in various parts of Australia. The police probably had a limited presence so racing on closed loops of roads became very popular. There were several courses in and around Bathurst including the Vale Circuit that could still be traced on the current road network.

So off we went in Matilda and to the north of town, not far from the modern racetrack, we found a sign on a pole indicating the start of the old Vale Circuit. The road led out into the countryside, past the local dog pound, wiggled over a stream and up to a T-junction. Here we turned right and the road twisted downhill before heading up steeply through some easy bends, a tighter one having been straightened out at some time in the past.

Now the current road turned to gravel, more like the whole track would have been back in the 1930s, over a hill where the riders were said to get airborne, a tight right and left turn, then up hill and down again before a sharp hairpin right onto a main road, now tarmac, and back towards the start.

The whole track would have been gravel in the old days of racing, and apparently the road was divided in two so the public could get access to viewing places while the racing took place on the other half of the road; don't tell Bernie Ecclestone or the safety committee of the Grand Prix Drivers' Association! For me, it was a great treat to sample roads previously used as race tracks and I wish we'd had time to try a couple of other former tracks in the area. They will have to wait until another visit.

We ventured into town and took a walk through a main park visiting a beautiful display of begonias in a glasshouse. The blooms were very impressive with strong and vibrant pinks, yellows and oranges. Nearby, we came upon the local equivalent of the Hollywood Walk of Fame – a series of plaques set into the pavement dedicated to various race drivers who had won The Great Race on the Mt Panorama circuit. These included Rauno Aaltonen, a great rally driver, Jacky Ickx, who also won Le Mans six times, and Peter Brock, perhaps Australia's greatest ever driver, who sadly died on a car rally when his car hit a tree.

Off again on a short drive of only 60 km (37 miles), and the chance to take a look at another former race track. Orange, a town similar to Bathurst, is the site of the Gnoo Blas circuit used for cars and bikes in the 1950s and was where Jack Brabham earned his stripes before getting into Formula 1. We took a drive around and had a look round the town where Pam spent rather too long in a Salvation Army charity shop. She is a charity shopaholic, and while we were in Australia never missed an opportunity to visit the Ozzie equivalent, an Op Shop (opportunity shop), or Vinnies, the St Vincent de Paul charity shops.

Orange was once a candidate to become the capital of Australia, before a decision was made to create Canberra. The town is also the birthplace of Banjo Paterson who wrote *Waltzing Matilda*, so we considered it appropriate to visit the remains of his birthplace in a park that bears his name.

We were heading generally west with no particular plan other than to head into the rural and remote areas of north-west NSW and Parkes was our next stop, but not before we took a break for coffee at Manildra, a small community dominated by huge flour mills. After our refreshment, we took a walk round the local roads and came upon the *Amusu* (amuse you) cinema, an old building which was the first cinema in Australia, one that remains in occasional use to this day. It is serendipitous finds like this that made a trip such as ours so enjoyable; you never know what's around the next corner.

Elvis lives

Once in Parkes, as always, we headed for the Visitor Information Centre, and next door were a couple of museums. A local man had built up a substantial collection of Elvis Presley artefacts and memorabilia, and donated it all to the town. We looked round the exhibits viewing some of Presley's cars, TVs, costumes, gold discs and much more. There was also a vast open air display of agricultural and commercial vehicles and equipment, and I wandered round trying to ignore the heat.

Nearby is the Parkes Radio Telescope, a noted astronomical research establishment with a 64m (210ft) receiving dish. We learned that there was to be entertainment there that evening with a musical combo, *Ologism*, playing rock music and carrying out various live scientific demonstrations. We would be able to get a meal and decided it was worth a try, so we booked a table.

It was dark by the time we got there and we joined a gathering to enjoy listening to the group, have a bit of a dance, and see the dish all lit up in an orange glow. The evening didn't really live up to expectations as the locals, most of whom seemed to work at the site, weren't too friendly and the food wasn't up to much; but it was something different. The band were the best part of the evening and their science tricks involving smoke, water and various other features were very clever.

A couple of weeks previously, I had bought a copy of the local edition of *Top Gear* magazine, and there was an article about a display of utility vehicle trucks at Ootha, not too far away. Utes, as they are more commonly known, are best described as the local equivalent of builders trucks in the UK, a cab with a flatbed at the rear to hold materials. They are very common across all of Australia and not all of them are used for commercial purposes.

At Ootha, some wise guy has drawn together about 20 old utes and various artists and sculptors have converted them into works of art and displayed them in a paddock. A cynical viewer might describe it as a decorative scrapyard, but they were all tastefully created and made to look like recognisable objects such as kangaroo, a Bundaberg rum bottle, and much more. Worth a side trip if one is in the area.

I had also learned about the Condo 750, a Dakar Rally-style event that was due to take place in a week's time in Condobolin, so we headed there to find out more. Condobolin was a small town on the Lachlan River serving the local agricultural community. The rally was the main event of the year and would see about 50 enduro motor bikes and 30 rally cars covering about 960 km (600 miles) in the area to the north of town over two days. Most of the route would be on private land with timed special stages along farm tracks, through woodland, and some very tricky and rough terrain.

This was just my cup of tea. I have taken part in many car rallies, including some in a 4x4, and Pam and I had previously competed in a long distance endurance rally in South America, some of it through terrain now used in the real Dakar Rally. We made ourselves known to the organisers of the Condo 750, told them of our experience and said we would spend a few days travelling round and come back for the event.

The Long Paddock

The next day, we headed off westward again and were soon travelling along the gravel Lachlan Valley Way heading towards the small community of Booligal when we saw a strange sight. Ahead was a cloud of dust above the road and at first we thought a road train was heading our way, but as we drew closer all we saw were thousands of sheep steadily trudging along towards us. They were all across the road and adjoining verges, which were quite wide, and they moved forward in total silence.

We stopped to watch, and a young chap on a motorbike approached us and we chatted. It seems farmers have the right to apply to run their sheep or cattle on the Long Paddock, the wide verges that exist along all of the roads. The animals can eat the grass, so it doesn't need cutting, and can be fattened up for free before being taken to what is euphemistically called the 'meatworks'.

He explained there are certain rules to be followed. They must have at least two shepherds in attendance all the time, usually one at the front and one at the back, warning signs must be put out along the roadside, and they must cover at least 10 km (6 miles) each day. There were 4,500 sheep in the flock that was passing us, and they had been on the road for six weeks and would be travelling for a couple more, before meeting their doom and ending up as lamb chops.

The Long Paddock idea, in effect the long field, seemed a great idea as both the highway authority and the farmers gained. The verges are really wide and need to be kept trim, so what better way? We would later see several herds of cattle on the Long Paddock accompanied by farmers keeping an eye on their charges.

We stopped at Booligal for coffee at the roadhouse. It was a tiny community of about 25 houses and we were tempted to return the following Saturday as they were planning to hold a sheep racing day. It sounded like it would be a great day, but for us the rally was a more attractive proposition. After our coffee, it was a straightforward drive south to Hay, the local regional town where we planned to stay for a few days.

To the north of Hay is a huge, totally flat area, supposedly the largest on the planet. The land does not follow the curvature of the Earth, and we were told it offered a great sunset, so we drove up there and stayed a couple of hours, and although we enjoyed a few glasses of wine while watching the sun go down, the sunset was good, but fairly average.

During World War II, Hay was taken over as a prisoner of war camp, so we took a look at a small museum set up in a couple of ancient railway carriages at the site of the old railway station. The town must have taken on the air of a huge prison in those times as there were thousands of inmates, starting with German and Italian internees, and then prisoners of war. Many trusties were allowed to work locally and benefitted the surrounding communities, with many staying on at the end of hostilities.

The town is at the junction of three of Australia's major highways, the Sturt, Cobb and Mid-Western, so it is a regular stopover for the long-distance trucks that criss-cross Australia and there were many huge lorries around. Just north of the main junction is a bridge over the Murrumbidgee River, the only one for miles around. It is regularly used by animals, such as the huge flock of sheep we had seen a few days ago, as it is part of a long-standing stock route. The stockman with the sheep we had seen told us they had brought all the sheep over the bridge and up the High Street a week before we saw them. There is even a sign on the bridge forbidding use of the bridge by stock without 24 hours' notice to the local police.

We were in the middle of the major sheep rearing region in Australia and the life of sheep shearers, legendary figures in Australian culture, is celebrated at Shearer Outback, a modern museum and interpretive centre. We took a visit which was all very interesting, the highlight being a shearing demonstration. Whilst the work is vital to the agricultural economy, shearing is very hard, strenuous work. For many years, the shearing cutters have been electrically powered and a half-decent shearer can remove a fleece from a sheep in about three minutes. Teams of shearers travel the Outback roaming from station to station to work the sheep and we had met a couple of them on our last trip to Australia.

We were motoring down the Darling River Run in a hire car, and, after struggling through a flooded road, arrived at the tiny community of Tilpa. In the small, tin shack pub were two shearers, bored out of their minds as they were due to travel to a nearby sheep station, but despite having a fully equipped 4x4, were held up by the flooded roads. They had been there for three days, and whilst the pub was getting good business from them, they would rather have been earning. They told us they were paid on a piece rate and were losing money.

Back at the Hall of Fame, we learned that despite much research, no adequate automated method to shear a sheep has yet been established. We found it a fascinating place.

It was time to make a leisurely return to Condobolin, but first we had a lunch date in Griffith. We had met a lovely couple in a campsite a few weeks back and they were keen to meet us again if we happened to be near their town. Griffith serviced the local fruit growing area and we found it to be a spacious and well laid out town. There is good reason for this as it was designed by Walter Burley Griffith, the architect who laid out Canberra. We had a good lunch with Bev and Bob and they told us about a holiday they had in Europe a few years previously. They were on a guided tour and had a code for the type of day they were to enjoy - an ABC day – another bloody church/castle/cathedral. I suppose that's the problem with having a long history, something they don't have in Australia.

Tennis history

After lunch, we headed for a small community at Barellan, home of Evonne Goolagong Cawley, one of the world's leading tennis players in the '70s and '80s. She won numerous Grand Slam tournaments, including two Wimbledon singles titles. As we were nearby, this visit was a must for Pam.

Many Australian towns have a large feature at the entrance to the town that represents some major moment of fame or the significance of the area, and on this occasion it was a 30 foot high tennis racket. Goolagong had Aboriginal origins and normally would not have had an opportunity to play tennis, but a resident had seen her interest and encouraged her to play. She practiced for hours against a wall at the town tennis club, which still exists. I took Pam's photo alongside the wall as well as by the huge tennis racket.

Our *Camps 6* directory of free and cheap campsites recommended nearby Tullibigeal where one could stop in the middle of the community near a pub. We found the spot alongside what counted as the local park, a dusty patch of sparse grass with a few pieces of children's play equipment, and next to an electricity supply and toilets which we could use. The community, like so many in these parts, sits in the shadow of huge grain silos, and as we parked up, a train arrived to load up grain. It chugged into the siding, blocking the road to the pub for about an hour while it loaded up each wagon, repositioned the power unit at the front and then chuntered away again.

By now, we were ready for our beer so went over the road to have a drink with the locals. As usual, we were well received and they wanted to know all about us. They were real characters living in a remote and isolated part of NSW and it must have been something of an event for two Brits to arrive. One of the locals looked like a leprechaun; he was quite small, had a long, dark beard, and a bashed-up, Australian bush hat. It was a great evening.

In the morning, we took a walk round the only shop in the village. It had been forced to close down some years before, but was reopened when the locals took it over as a community project and now stocked just about everything one could think of; I've never seen axe head wedges for sale in B&Q.

Condo 750

When we returned to Condobolin, it was a hub of activity getting ready for the rally. Rather than park up at the town's campsite, we joined the rally fraternity in the showground where there were already dozens of cars, service vehicles, bikes, caravans and motorhomes parked up. We set up shop and actually found a power outlet to hook up to, which helped, and then took a look at the vehicles getting ready for the rally.

The bikes were all enduro-style with navigation units fitted on the handlebars that would take the rolls of route instructions written up in Tulip form, a standard format for rallies. The cars varied from near standard 4x4s, to well-known models highly modified to take part in rallies, and specialist dune buggy-type cars. There were also a few quad bikes.

The service and support vehicles were also very varied. One had actually been to South America for the Dakar Rally and still carried the decals from that event. Entrants and support vehicles had come from all over Australia for the event; one crew I spoke to had brought a flatbed truck loaded with their rally car in a four-day continuous drive from Perth, taking it in turns to drive while others slept.

We made ourselves known to the organiser and Geoff, the motor club president, took us under his wing and arranged for us to help marshalling the first stage of the event the next morning. He supplied us with maps and a copy of the official road book that the cars would be using, so we could make our way around the route to watch and marshal.

In the evening, all the vehicles were driven up to the main street of the town for scrutineering, checks to ensure they met safety standards, and the correct criteria for the class they were entered in. It was a rather casual affair compared to that in the UK, but the basics were covered. The entrants were then displayed for the townsfolk to see them and the locals had a chance to get autographs. There was a great atmosphere and sense of anticipation for the weekend ahead.

It was an early start for us as we needed to be in position well before the first competitor came along. We had been asked to go to the end of the first special stage about 10 km (6 miles) out of town. It would be tackled by the bikes today and the cars tomorrow. We found the track and headed down until we reached a crossroads which would mark the end of the first stage. The stage commander asked if we could do the timekeeping.

No problem for us as we had plenty of experience, so we parked up Matilda at the stage stop point and another marshal headed to the flying finish point about 75 metres (80 yards) away: we would communicate using the CB radio, the first time we would used it. Pam took the official timing clock and I stood where the bikes would come to a stop after crossing the flying finish. I would take their time card, hand it to Pam to mark the time on it, and then hand it back to the rider, who would then head on to the next stage.

It wasn't long before we could hear the first bike in the distance. He appeared at great speed amid masses of dust and headed towards us and I waved him down to stop. There was dust everywhere, the bike smelt hot, the rider's eyes were 'in the zone' and he was still high on his first dose of adrenalin for the day. I was enjoying it as much as he was.

Within moments, the next bike arrived, then the next, and before long they had all been through, about 60 motorbikes, none with any problems. We had to wait another half hour until the time control officially closed, and by then we had packed up and were ready to go. Looking back at the crossroads, it was hard to see that anything had been going on, and it was still before 8.00 a.m.

Next, we had been asked to go to a marshalling point about 40 km (25 miles) away, so off we headed onto local gravel farm roads. Matilda wasn't that fast and we were soon passed by cars, bikes and service vehicles as they speeded along liaison sections between the timed special stages. One was the Dakar service truck and it sailed past us as we were doing 50 mph, so he was probably doing 70 mph+, not hanging about. It was great fun and we felt part of the whole shebang.

Our next post was a mid-stage point where the route crossed a public highway; in reality, a narrow farm road and with a gate that had to be opened and closed by each competitor as they passed through. Our job was to make sure any vehicles on the public highway stopped if a competitor was crossing, and generally keep the public in a safe place. That last task wasn't a problem as everyone was connected to the rally in some way so was well aware of where to stand and keep safe.

We had a long wait, but eventually we could see the first bike in the far distance flying along a distant track followed by a huge rooster tail of dust. The bike then seemed to come to a stop, probably a direction change through a gate, and then it crossed left to right in front of us, about half a mile away, again followed by a massive dust trail. And then it was heading towards us, the rider with his head down close to the handlebars to minimise drag, until he sat up and brought the bike to a stop right at the gate. The rider then had to unhook the latch, drive through and then close the gate, all without getting off the bike. He was waved across the highway and vanished along another track that led away from our point alongside a wood. More dust; we were soon filthy, covered from head to toe in red dust.

Already the next rider was in sight and in no time had come to a sliding stop at the gate, done the necessary and accelerated off into the distance. One followed another. There was more dust, the raucous noise of the bikes, the look of determination on the riders' faces – all sights and sounds I have experienced many times, but one I never tire of.

A course closing vehicle came by and told us the stage was finished so we headed on north to the halfway stop at Vermont Hill, a dilapidated, corrugated iron, village hall about 30 km (20 miles) away. Here all the competitors had a one-hour stop for food and a chance to service their vehicle. The area was peppered with cars, bikes and support trucks, many of the bikes on stands being worked on, the 4x4s on jacks with mechanics scrabbling around underneath.

The local Country Women's Association (the equivalent of the WI) were providing food and drink in the hall, and there was the usual crowd of onlookers, ourselves included. The difference for me was that I was in shorts and T-shirt and the temperature was about 38C, whereas in the UK a similar event would see me in numerous layers, anorak, reflective jacket, bobble hat and boots, standing in the middle of a Welsh forest in November. I know which I preferred!

We didn't have any marshalling to do in the afternoon so headed off to watch some of the cars and soon found a stage finish where the cars came through a wood, dipped into a ditch, up around a tree and on to the finish line. There were fewer cars, only about 25, but having rallied a 4x4 in South America myself, I was more interested in them.

As always, each car stopped at the finish line and the co-driver handed his time card out to a marshal and then got it back with his time for the stage recorded thereon. Often the driver would get out, dressed in fireproof overalls and helmet, and check around his vehicle for any obvious damage or problem. Then it was into the car, full harness clipped up, and off again with a sense of urgency so as to be at the next stage on time.

We saw all the cars through and then went off to find a stage start. Each car would arrive at a steady speed on a liaison section and turn in off the road to a gazebo where the marshals had their time keeping clocks. The co-driver would walk over with his time card and get a time to start the stage, usually in a couple of minute's time, allowing him and his driver to get ready. Once they were both ready, they would creep forward to the start line and the marshal, with his own handheld clock, would give them a 30-second signal, 10-second signal, and, as the last few seconds were called out, the revs would be built up. At 'Go', the tyres bit into the dust and gravel as the car sped away across the edge of a field and into a wood, followed by the inevitable rooster tail of dust.

We'd had a great day, or at least I had. Although Pam has been on lots of rallies, it is a bit under sufferance, but she had done some reading, chatted to various people and got very dirty.

Back at Condobolin showground, we used Matilda's shower, rather than queue for the rather scruffy public showers, had a bite to eat and wandered round the paddock to chat with competitors and various people we had met during the day. Tyres and shock absorbers were being changed, panels being bashed out, and once more the scene was of tired activity, getting ready for another set of stages.

In the morning, we went to a fresh stage for us and watched the start, walking in about 500 metres (550 yards) to photograph the cars taking a series of bends around a pond. Then it was back to the 'gate' stage, where there was a bigger crowd, and, once the cars started coming through, plenty of action. The cars arrived at the gate at full speed, braking hard in time to stop, let the co-driver out to work the gate, then close the gate again and speed off once he (or she) was belted in.

A couple of cars cried 'enough' as they reached the gate, one with engine problems, the other with unspecified suspension issues, so that added to the atmosphere.

For safety, the event organisers had the use of a helicopter, and this had been buzzing about on both days accompanied by a lorry with a fuel tank on the back. Our 'minder' Geoff was with this truck today and he called me over.

"We've got special security arrangements for the fuel today," he said.

"Security arrangements? Out here? What do you mean?" I asked and he beckoned me over to the truck.

On the back platform was a huge sack and he opened it up to reveal a 4 metres (12 ft) carpet python.

"Nobody's going to try and pinch the fuel with that on the back."

"Where on earth did you get that?"

"It was on the track near a stage start and it might have been run over so we put it up here. We'll find a safe place to let it go later on."

Although the python isn't venomous, it is a constrictor, and it looked huge and was plump, so was a well-fed specimen. Rather them than me. The only wildlife we had seen in the last couple of days were several blue-tongued lizards, usually about a metre (3 ft) long, but they usually scampered away into the bush as we drew near. And, yes, they do quite literally have blue tongues, although their bodies are browny-green as camouflage.

The rally finished a bit earlier today so everyone could get back to Condobolin in time for the dinner and prize giving. This was another friendly occasion and we chatted with tired competitors, supporters and spectators, one of whom we found out lived near our daughter in Manly.

The next morning, we moved back to the proper campsite so as to spend some time cleaning up Matilda, and ourselves. There was a thick layer of dust everywhere, inside and outside the motorhome. In particular, some cupboards had let in masses of the stuff and everything had to come out and be washed. Pam spent lots of time in the laundry room, whilst I took charge of the hose to wash Matilda.

A nice touch was that Geoff came round and asked how we had enjoyed ourselves and left us a couple of baseball caps from the event sponsor, Slattery Auctions.

The rally had been an unexpected diversion, one I wouldn't have missed for the world, but it was time to move on, as with our unexpected circuit of this part of NSW, we had spent ten days in the area, rather more than we had planned for.

On again

Clean and rested, we headed away from Condobolin and soon got some miles on the clock. We stopped for coffee at Westhalle, a trucker's stop, had a great brew of coffee, and the owner gave us both a slab of fruit cake usually only given to truckers: we felt honoured.

We didn't stop in Hay this time but joined the Sturt Highway and eventually we made it to Mildura, a big town, where we stopped at the BIG4 site after 720 km (450 miles). We were tired and weary. Before leaving Condobolin, we had stocked up on food, in particular fresh fruit and veg. This was a mistake as we learned that at the nearby border with South Australia, we would have to throw it all out unless it was cooked, frozen or eaten. There are heavy fines for anyone who contravenes the strict rules, designed to prevent the spread of pests and diseases. We didn't want to get into trouble so we had a big veggie meal, followed by fruit salad, after which we cut up and froze as much as we could.

The next day, we approached the border and, like everyone else, were subjected to a thorough search by Agricultural Inspectors. We drove into a check station, much like the old border controls that used to be a feature of European borders, and after asking a few questions, the inspector thoroughly checked Matilda over, inside and out, even the fridge and little freezer, now jam-packed. We passed and were allowed to go on, driving under a Dunlop tyre bridge that used to grace the Adelaide Formula 1 circuit. Welcome to South Australia.

I was very tired after the rally and the last few days' driving, so we stopped at the first town we came to, Renmark, and found a great campsite alongside the Murray River, Australia's major river and about 100 yards wide at this point.

Since leaving Sydney, Matilda had developed an annoying little fault; as we went round left-hand corners at any speed, one of the drawers under the worktop would slide out and crash to the floor. I had taken a look at the catch and checked out the runners, and whilst I had made some improvement, the problem persisted. The drawer was, however, quite big and heavy at about three feet long and nine inches deep, and I was concerned that one day it would break up, or crash into the sink unit on the other side of Matilda and damage a door.

The other problem was the grey water tank, the outlet to which had always leaked, leaving a small pool of water underneath Matilda whenever we stopped.

We headed into Renmark and found a caravan dealer, who took a look at the leak, applied some new hose, and copious quantities of glue and claimed it would do the trick. Fortunately, Sydney RV Centre agreed to pay the cost.

For the other problem, we were directed to a kitchen fitting showroom. The owner was very helpful and offered me a couple of lengths of worktop laminate that would build up the catch. It worked for a month or so, before we started to hear the familiar sound as the drawer crashed to the floor when going around left corners.

After a leisurely day in Renmark, which was a lovely, tidy town, and a couple of evenings watching glorious sunsets over the Murray River, we headed on, now in a more northerly direction and away from the vast plains we had been driving across in recent days.

A typical Australian scene with a wind powered Artesian well drawing water for livestock

The countryside became more rolling and Burra was our next stopping point; a pretty little town that reminded us of a Cotswold village. It sat in a valley with a river running through the centre of the town and had a small village green with a war memorial in the middle: very different to most Australian towns.

In the evening, we gave an Italian restaurant a try and it was a great find. The tables were laid out in what appeared to be the front room of a house, and rather than the usual piped music, customers could pick what they wanted from a collection of LPs and play them on an ancient record player. The grub was good too.

A stop for coffee in Peterborough led to us visiting the Visitor Information Centre and hearing about the history of the town when it was an important railway junction. The centre was in an old railway carriage and next door was a museum with more history of the town. In particular, we learned about Bob, a mongrel dog who used to travel on the trains all over Australia, but always made his way back to Peterborough. With the decline of the railways, the town had fallen into recession and, sadly, was rather run-down and seedy.

We drove on to Orroroo for the night, another run-down town. It was a Saturday and in the afternoon we took a walk round, but everything was closed, a major contrast to how our local High Street would be. As we were planning to head into more remote regions, we stayed an extra day while I checked over Matilda, did some bolt tightening, and generally made sure everything was up to par.

Into the Flinders Range

The plan was to take a look at the Flinders Range, so we drove up to Hawker and on to the Wilpena Pound Information Centre. We had hoped to take a look at Wilpena Pound itself, a huge natural amphitheatre set in this mountainous region, a hefty walk up from the centre. Unfortunately, we couldn't book a campsite, and, as we were in a national park, couldn't free camp, so we decided to press on north. Looking back, I suspect we should have tried harder, as the natural bowl of the Pound is very spectacular. Next time.

We headed off the tarmac onto various 4x4 roads and saw all manner of wildlife including the local version of the wallaby, the yellow back. We were lucky to see one as it was right by the road and was well camouflaged with its surroundings. We stopped at the Razorback Lookout viewpoint, which gave a gorgeous view over the surrounding countryside and the distant jagged mountain tops (as shown on the front cover of this book).

We eventually made it to Blinman, a former mining community, but, with the mines closed, was having to rely on passing tourists for its economic survival. We had some tea in the old schoolroom, now a café, as all the local children were now receiving their education via the School of the Air. A piece of land just outside the village had been set aside for free camping so we set up shop for the night and enjoyed the complete silence; it was quite eerie.

I would have liked to have headed on north through various 4x4 roads and then onto the long Strzelecki Desert Track. However, both of us had had enough of the dust that would accompany such a trip, and anyway, we had another 4x4 track lined up to try, so we decided to head west to the main road north via the Parachilna Gorge. This unsurfaced track was a spectacular drive, often running along the dried up creek bed, at other times twisting in and out of eucalyptus trees. At its narrowest, the gorge is only a few yards wide, so the road must be closed at times when the river flows, but it was very dry when we went through with only a few puddles to negotiate.

Feral food

The gorge led us out of the national park on a track that was very corrugated, a regular problem on Australian tracks, to the small community of Parachilna itself. There was little here except the Prairie Hotel, which has had many notable guests including Kate Winslet, Russell Crowe and others. The Flinders region offers plenty of great film locations, as does Lake Torrens to the west, and the arid land all around, so the hotel is often used as a base for film crews. Major feature films such as *Gallipoli* and *Rabbit-Proof Fence* were filmed here.

The hotel is also famous for serving 'feral food', delicacies such as kangaroo, wallaby, emu, wild pork and camel. I had to try some so ordered a camel sausage roll which was, as one might expect, very gamey.

In the bar, I noticed they sold Fargher lager, and the logo for the brew was the Three Legs of Man, obviously very familiar to me. The story was that the pub was originally a normal run-down roadhouse until 1991 when Jane and Ross Fargher, who lived on a nearby station and were descendants of a Manxman, bought their 'local' and subsequently developed it into what it is today. When they started to develop their own brew, they decided to use the three legs logo. It was a long way from the Isle of Man but nice to see the logo in a very unexpected and remote place.

As always, there was roadkill along the road, and whereas we would normally see kites pulling a carcase apart, for the first time we saw a wedgy, a wedge-tailed eagle, hard at work. Normally as we approached roadkill (a regular occurrence), kites would have no problem reacting to us bearing down on them by flying away well before we reached the carcase. However, eagles are much bigger and this one struggled to get into the air, and but for some heavy braking, we might have had a dead, or even worse, an injured eagle, on our bull bar. He made it – just.

We now headed north over familiar ground through Leigh Creek to Marree, a town we had visited before after coming down the Birdsville Track. We checked into the rather basic campsite and headed over to the hotel for an evening there chatting to Andy, the Essex lad we had met previously.

The Oodnadatta Track

Whereas our journey down the Birdsville Track to Marree was unremarkable and we saw hardly anyone, our trip up the nearby Oodnadatta Track was to be quite different. The Birdsville was developed from an old cattle droving track used by cattlemen from Queensland to get their cattle to the railhead that existed at Marree. The Oodnadatta came into existence when the railway was extended north from Marree towards Alice Springs. This was on the west side of Lake Eyre and the plan was to open up the heart of Australia and create a north/south link with Darwin. Because the territory through which the railway passed was so hostile, the engineers chose to follow ancient Aboriginal trading routes via numerous mound springs in the region.

These springs were vital to the Aborigines as they provided a water supply in otherwise very remote and arid areas. One can see several beside the track, low mounds of rock through which springs discharge water through narrow fissures, in many cases creating small ponds surrounded by plants; in fact, something like a desert oasis. A disadvantage of the springs is that they attract some of the slithery nasties found in the desert, in particular venomous snakes, so take care if you go and investigate them.

The engineers also recruited Afghan workers to do the hard work and these, in turn, brought with them camels for transport purposes.

This led to several developments. Once the railway was built, the camels were no longer needed and were let loose to roam the Outback, which led to the huge population of camels that now exists in the Outback. Another side effect was the introduction of the kapok tree to Australia. This yellow flowering tree can be found all over the north of Australia and its origins lie in the saddles the Afghan workers brought with them for their camels. The saddles were stuffed with kapok filler and the seeds eventually found their way into the soil and flourished.

The Oodnadatta Track follows this railway line, the original Ghan, for several hundred miles passing the derelict remains of railway infrastructure such as trestle bridges, stations and water towers. About 200 km (125 miles) from Marree is the small community of William Creek where a road joins from the west and Cooper Pedy, and then another 240 km (150 miles) further on is the small town of Oodnadatta with its famous Pink Roadhouse. Here there are various options and rather than continue on gravel roads to Alice Springs via Finke, we chose to head north-west to the Stuart Highway at Marla, yet another 240 km (150 miles).

We made a prompt start from our caravan site in Marree and headed to the general store to fuel up. Like many Outback towns, there is only one shop and this one acted as Post Office, café, grocer, clothes shop, camping shop, and more.

Next door was a typical Outback oddity – the Lake Eyre Yacht Club. Ninety per cent of the time, Lake Eyre, the southern end of which is about 90 km (60 miles) away, is a dried up salt lake. Sir Donald Campbell used the smooth dry surface of the lake to set a new World Land Speed Record of 403.1mph (648.72kph) in July 1964. However, once in a while, maybe every ten years or so, there is sufficient rain to turn the hard, sun-baked surface into a proper lake, and then the locals take full advantage and sail their boats. Only in Australia!

Leaving town, and the tarmac, we stopped at the large road sign that provides information on the state of the roads, and it confirmed all the roads ahead were open. We were soon heading north up the track with signs of the former railway line passing us at regular intervals. Just outside town are the remains of a 100 yard length of trestle that originally took the track across a dry creek. The structure was in a surprisingly good condition, although the metal rails have long gone. We stopped at various old railway halts, sidings, viaducts and water towers, and then came upon the next oddity - Plane Henge.

Melbourne artist Robin Cooke, who has a house alongside the track, has built a collection of large metal artworks that stand out in the desert. Inevitably, we had to stop and look. Most notable is Plane Henge, inspired by Stonehenge back in the UK, consisting of two upended Beechcraft light aircraft. Nearby are other smaller works, and a few miles up the road is a remodelled bus named the Ghan Hover-bus.

We travelled on, Matilda running well on the graded gravel surface. Traffic was intermittent with the occasional camper van or 4x4 and camping trailer heading the other way, reassuring if we were to need help at some time.

Gradually, we could begin to see the edge of Lake Eyre South, a spur of the main lake, on our right side – an incredibly bright, white flat pan, edged with dull, brown vegetation. We stopped for a few minutes at a purpose-built view spot with information boards and chatted to a young couple heading the other way. They reported that the track was in good condition and they had suffered no punctures.

On rejoining the track, we soon saw our first dingo. Dingoes have become (in)famous in the Australian psyche as a result of the tragic baby Azaria Chamberlain case. In 1980, the Chamberlain family were camping near Uluru when nine-week-old Azaria was snatched by a dingo and never found. A long and involved series of court cases followed and the baby's mother, Lindy, was subsequently imprisoned for murder, and it was some years before a second coroner confirmed the baby had indeed been taken by a dingo. Lindy Chamberlain, the mother, subsequently received a pardon.

Prior to the Chamberlain case, the Australian public had a benevolent opinion of dingoes and it was considered impossible that they would take a baby, a view that did not help the Chamberlain's case when it came to court. Now the potential impact of dingoes on people has changed somewhat as they have been known to take other children and kill them, notably a young boy at Fraser Island, off Queensland. Here there is a significant population of dingoes, supposedly the most pure-bred because of their isolation on the island. The problem lies in the similarity of dingoes to domestic dogs and the public's perception that they can be approached, offered food and generally treated as if they were pet dogs.

The dingo we came upon was a very emaciated and sick dog that showed no fear of Matilda and wandered right up to us in the hope, I guess, of being offered some food. With the drought conditions in Central Australia, we had heard that many wild animals were suffering and we both felt very sorry for this poor wretch who could hardly walk and was clearly in some pain. Sadly, we were forced to leave him to his fate as the general advice was not to feed dingoes or any other wild animal.

Normally, when the road was smooth(ish), we could safely travel at about 80-100 kph (50-60 mph), and we were bowling along a few miles later when I realised there was a large snake in the road. I passed over it and came to a prompt stop and reversed back to take a closer look. Like most people, I have a fear of snakes, but this is accompanied by a fascination with them. Not being knowledgeable on Australian snakes and knowing several varieties were highly venomous, I wasn't going to get too close so Pam stayed in the motorhome while I took some photographs - with my telephoto lens from a safe distance!

Australia is home to several of the top ten most venomous snakes on the planet and whilst there are other non-venomous snakes resident on the continent, we weren't going to take any chances. As it turned out, we were right to treat it with great caution as we showed our photographs to the staff at the Reptile Centre in Alice Springs a few days later and they confirmed it to be a western brown, more properly known these days as a mulga snake, but second most venomous in the world. We drove on.

Soon, we came to a right turning to Coward Springs, a caravan site set up around a hot water spring and former stop on the old Ghan railway. The caravan park owner is renovating the old railway buildings and in one was a small museum of local artefacts, photos and documents so we had a look. We had no plans to stay for the night, especially after seeing a sign that stated, *"Campers – it's REPTILE weather. Use a torch at night."* We did, however, take the opportunity to try out the springs. Hot water rises from underground and feeds a small pool not much bigger than a domestic bath, although it is much deeper. It was lovely and refreshing, but, with the reptile warning, we drove on again after our pleasant soaking.

William Creek

Not long before reaching our target for the day, William Creek, we came to the turning where a 80 km (50 miles) track heads out east towards Halligan's Bay on Lake Eyre. It is the site of an Outback tragedy that serves as a warning to all who travel the remote regions of Australia. Back in 1998, two Austrian tourists travelling in a Britz Trooper camper van headed out on the track from William Creek and got bogged down in loose sand on the edge of the lake. They had left word at William Creek that they would be a few days and had taken plenty of food and water, in addition to which they were bogged next to a large water tank and shelter.

Tragically, a mix-up at the hotel meant no one was aware they were missing, and after a couple of days the tourists decided they had been forgotten and gathered together water and a tent to try and walk out. As an experienced walker and a medical student, Caroline Grossmueller reckoned they could walk most of the way back at night so as to avoid the daytime heat of 40C+. The temperature turned out to be much warmer at night than they anticipated (about 38C) and progress was slow. They drank more water than expected, and eventually Caroline's partner, Karl, decided to stay in the tent while she walked on.

Sadly, she never made it and her body was found a few days later, only a few yards from a cattle trough with ample water. Karl was rescued and a local policeman had no trouble driving the Trooper out of the sand after letting the tyre pressures down to 24 psi. An inquest found that the couple had good information with them about the dangers of the Outback and how to respond when in difficulty, yet it seemed they hadn't taken them on board. There is now a monument on the track to commemorate Caroline's tragic death. Advice to 4x4 hirers has also improved and recording systems at Outback locations are now better managed.

The inquest noted several points of advice should one find oneself in a similar situation:

- Stay with the vehicle

- Stay in the shade

- Conserve water

- Prepare signals - e.g. fire, mirror, and ground markings that can be seen by search aircraft

- Carry recovery gear.

We arrived in William Creek during the late afternoon, checked into the caravan site and soon got yarning with a couple of families travelling together with camping trailers. William Creek is hardly the centre of the universe, comprising the pub and caravan site, an airstrip and a few dwellings. That's all. Its raison d'être is to offer accommodation and fuel to travellers on the track and offer flights over nearby Lake Eyre from the airstrip.

The little community lies in the middle at Anna Creek Station, at 6,000,000 acres and about the size of Israel, the largest cattle ranch in the world and may have up to 15,000 to 20,000 cattle.

Anna Creek was part of the Kidman empire, more properly S. Kidman and Co., cattle ranchers. Although Anna Creek is huge, the vast cattle business started in the nineteenth century by Sydney Kidman is one of the largest private land holdings on the planet and I had been reading a biography of Kidman during our travels.

Sydney Kidman was of English descent, his family emigrating from Suffolk to settle in Adelaide. He was born in May 1857 but left home when only 13 years old to seek work eventually ending up in the Barrier Ranges around Broken Hill where in addition to cattle work he became involved in the evolving mining industry.

In the 1880s, Kidman saw his future in the cattle industry and sold his shares in the Broken Hill Mining Company to invest in cattle stations and a carting company. This was a decision he would later regret as Broken Hill later became BHP Billiton, one of the largest and richest mining companies worldwide.

However, Kidman flourished in his own right with his carting company expanding across New South Wales and Queensland, and later into Western Australia competing with Cobb and Co., the other major company in the industry. Alongside it was the cattle empire that grew and grew mainly in and around the Channel Country of central Australia as he bought up cattle stations across the country and became Australia's leading cattle baron.

In fact, we had been travelling across Kidman country when we crossed through Queensland early in our trip through Winton, Middleton and Birdsville. Coincidentally, Nicole Kidman, the actress, is a descendant of Sydney Kidman and appeared in the film *Australia* as a cattle rancher.

Once we had set up, we headed into the pub for a couple of cold beers and pay our fee for the pitch. The bar was busy with travellers and some of the pilots who fly the tourist planes over the lake. Most were female and none over 25 years old, but they were mad about flying and having obtained their private pilot's licence, the most basic form of licence, they come to places like William Creek to fly tourist planes. This builds up their flying hours so to become eligible to start training for their commercial pilot's licence.

At the bar, I realised I had lost my credit card. Now the Outback is not the place to lose a credit card – how does one get a replacement sent to you? We checked everywhere, in Matilda, my clothing and anywhere we could think of, and finally we reckoned I may have left it at the general store at Marree when I bought petrol. We faced a 250 mile round-trip back down there, and then back up to William Creek, so first I phoned the shop and spoke to the owner.

"Yes. I have it here; you left it in the cash machine. You're not the only traveller to do that."

"Thanks. However, I am now at William Creek and don't fancy a 250 mile round-trip to collect it. Could you give it to someone coming up the track tomorrow and I'll wait for them here?"

"I have a better and more reliable idea. Speak to Trevor; he runs the tourist flights over the lake. He has a pilot coming down tomorrow to pick up a couple of tourists staying at the Marree Hotel and take them out over the lake. Ask the pilot to pick up your card and he can bring it back to you when he flies back to William Creek."

This sounded like a much better idea, so later in the hotel bar I tracked down Trevor, a typical Outback guy with a checked shirt, battered bush hat, and as large as life. It turned out he had recently purchased the hotel and also owned numerous aircraft flying over the lake and other nearby locations. I explained the problem.

"That's OK. Jarod is taking a plane down to Marree tomorrow for a lake trip and then coming back. Have a word with him. Better than that, there are several spare seats in the plane. Why don't you go down with him, get your card and have a coffee? He'll be a couple of hours and then you can come back with him and be back before lunch."

This sounded great, but I gave a hesitant cough and asked, "Is there room for two so my wife can join us?"

"Sure, no problem. Enjoy the trip."

We didn't need to discuss the matter further. Amazingly, Trevor didn't want anything for it, although I bought him a beer. I then spoke to Jarod, who seemed to be the only male pilot around and the only one more than 30 years old, and arranged a meeting time in the morning.

Dawn was just starting to break as we wandered over to the airstrip to meet Jarod at 6.30 a.m. and help him get the aircraft out of the hangar and ready for the flight. Soon after we taxied across the road, which until recently was actually used as the landing strip, to the tarmac runway. Then it was up and away on our way to Marree, yet again. Soon, we could see a fine line drawn in the arid land below, the old railway track tracing a faint path back south, and to the east the edge of Lake Eyre with its white expanse stretching toward the rising sun. It was an amazing sight.

All too soon, actually about 40 minutes, we were lining up to land at Marree and Jarod arranged a lift into town for us; it was a couple of miles away, too far to walk in this environment. We went to the store and retrieved the card - it was one of several lying in a drawer under the till - and had some breakfast. We had a look round Marree again and found out that there were still descendants of the original Afghan workers living in the town, and even a mosque, although it was now a dilapidated, straw-roofed structure with crumbling stone walls.

We also looked round the old railway station, rather more substantial than others we had seen yesterday. There were also a couple of old, diesel engine, power units and some railway carriages slowly rusting away and in a very sorry state.

We wandered over to the hotel for a coffee and another chat with Andy, and it wasn't long before Jarod appeared ready to head back. The return flight was just as good and we were back in the pub by 11.30 a.m. to thank Trevor once more before packing up the van and setting off towards Oodnadatta. RESULT - a great treat and no cost to us!

A couple of cyclists pedalling away on the Oodnadatta Track was not something we expected to see

As we headed north, the condition of the track gradually deteriorated with quite a lot of loose gravel and sand on the road. This slowed us somewhat, but suddenly we started seeing the wheel tracks of what appeared to be bicycles. Low and behold, not far ahead we came upon two cyclists slowly making their way through some soft sand that happened to cover the track at this point. I slowed right down so as to avoid caking them in more dust and we stopped to chat.

They were covered head to toe with protection against the harsh sun and their faces were also covered with a face net, a standard item of Outback clothing also known jokingly as the Australian burka, to keep the flies away.

It turned out they had cycled up from Adelaide - that's over 1,000 km (630 miles) - and were heading to Alice Springs, a further 675 km (420 miles), after which one of them, a 75-year-old, was cycling on to Darwin – yet another 1,520 km (950 miles) although the going would be better if he stuck to the Stuart Highway. After we had topped up their water bottles, we headed on our way: and people back home thought we were mad to attempt our trip!

Pink Roadhouse

The Pink Roadhouse at Oodnadatta is an Outback icon. In 1974, Adam Plate and his partner took the roadhouse over and set about promoting the area as a potential tourist destination with innovative ideas that attracted attention. Notable amongst these was to paint the roadhouse pink so that for evermore Oodnadatta would be associated with its Pink Roadhouse, and Plate also set about erecting signs at all the road junctions and other key points in the area to help visitors find their way to his establishment. These signs were simple, hand-painted on what appeared to be old dustbin lids, and we had seen a few as we motored along.

Adam Plate is also credited with giving the track its name as he felt that with a proper name, like the Birdsville Track and Strzelecki Track, it would become a proper destination in itself.

Plate became a stalwart of the area and was widely recognised for the work he had undertaken to attract visitors and increase tourism in this remote part of the Outback. Sadly, however, he was another rally driver to hit a tree and suffer fatal injuries, this on a rally near Adelaide in 2012.

We had planned to stay in Oodnadatta, so after a coffee in the famous roadhouse, we took a tour of the small town but found it to be very run-down and the caravan site was none too pleasant. We decided to drive on and free camp further up the road, and after passing side turnings to Finke and Dalhousie Springs, eventually pulled up at a dried up creek crossing near Todmorden Station.

It was dark by now and soon we could hear dingoes howling in the night. After we had eaten, I sat outside for a while and gazed in wonderment at the stars. It took a while for my eyes to adjust to the darkness, but soon I could see the whole of the Milky Way laid out above me as a swathe of stars stretching from horizon to horizon. There were yet more stars behind and the astonishing picture was something I hadn't seen before with such clarity – quite amazing – and it made one realise how minuscule Earth is within the immensity of the Universe. It was something I would do a few more times during the trip; it isn't possible in Europe because of the impact of artificial light.

We were woken by a passing vehicle at about 6.30 a.m. and by the dingoes that were still being vocal. Within an hour, we had packed up and headed off on the last part of the Oodnadatta Track to Marla on the Stuart Highway. The track was much rougher, especially at the creek crossings, all of which were dried up, with the road surface cut up with large, loose rocks and stones. Care was necessary to avoid punctures.

As we came close to Marla, the road improved and our speed increased, and suddenly there were three kangaroos on the track in front of us. I started slowing and two of them dashed off into the bush on the right, the third darting left across the track directly in front of us. I just missed him, but then one of the others decided to follow and we just missed him too as he flashed past. Inevitably, the third 'roo decided to join his mates and all of a sudden he flew out of the bushes and headed across the road, but fortunately for him we were now driving very slowly and he crossed safely. The incident highlighted the problem with wild animals and why so much roadkill can be seen alongside many of the Outback roads.

The major Outback tracks have informative signs warning of road conditions ahead. This one was seen at the northern end of the Oodnadatta Track

We reached Marla by mid-morning and assessed the state of Matilda. The tyres looked alright and now that we would be running back on tarmac, I pumped them up to normal running pressures again. We also treated ourselves to a cooked breakfast in the café. The real issue was the red dust, as once again inside Matilda it was everywhere – in cupboards, on the soft furnishings and there was a fine layer over the worktops. Oh, joy!

Alice Springs

We faced another 480 km (300 miles) to Alice Springs all on the Stuart Highway which was quite busy, certainly when compared to the remote driving we had been doing in recent weeks. We stopped briefly at the roadhouses at Kulgera and Erldunda, the latter being very busy as it is at the main junction for the road to Uluru, Kings Canyon and Kata Tjuta (The Olgas). Finally, we stopped for a few days' rest at the BIG4 campsite just outside Alice Springs. We were ready for the rest, and Alice offered some attractions to visit, plus we needed to spend some time cleaning up Matilda and making sure the mechanicals were alright.

Alice Springs lies hard up against the MacDonnell Range of hills where the Todd River has long ago carved a narrow gap through which the Stuart Highway and the modern Ghan railway pass. The town is a busy regional centre, and although it is a long way to anywhere it attracts a lot of tourists, most of whom fly in as a jump off point for Uluru.

Not many people realise how far it is to Uluru from Alice, as when looking at the average packaged holiday brochure, or even an A4 size map of the continent, the town of Alice and Uluru look to be adjacent to each other. In fact, it is 560 km (350 miles), the distance from central London to Glasgow, with few refuelling opportunities and hardly any communities, although the road is now tarmac. And, of course, it is then another 560 km (350 miles) back to Alice.

Supposedly people often turn up at the taxi rank at the airport and ask to be taken to Uluru. I am not sure many taxi drivers would do the trip, but it would be a good earner if they did. For the independent traveller, there are coach trips from the town that will take you there and back in a day, but they start very early in the morning and don't get back until very late at night. Nor do they leave much time to see the monolith in the desert that attracts so many people.

For us, our first priority was to give Matilda the once over again. Pam spent yet another day clearing out the dust from the inside and I cleaned up the exterior. I also checked it over mechanically and found, as I had suspected for a day or two, that the rear exhaust box was breaking away. We soon found an exhaust centre to fix that.

We had decided to spend a week in Alice and took the opportunity to be proper tourists and visit a few of the attractions, one of which was the Desert Park. This was an open site where the complex natural systems of the desert were explained, dry river beds, swamps, water holes, woodlands, sand lands, and more. It involved quite a bit of walking around guided routes, fortunately on a day that was relatively cool. At various places around the park were aviaries with many colourful birds, some of which we had already seen, and there was also an underground nocturnal house which offered an insight into the lives of the more secretive creatures of the desert. Here were glass-fronted enclosures with mammals, reptiles and invertebrates, including bilbies and mala, marsupials rarely seen in the wild. We enjoyed a couple of presentations from guides, one on medicines derived from desert plants, the other featuring flying displays of various birds of the desert. We also took a walk through an enclosure of red kangaroos. The place is well worth a visit.

Life for pioneers in the remote Outback was very hard and we had learned about some of this in Longreach at The Stockman's Hall of Fame. Here in Alice was the National Pioneer Women's Hall of Fame, a smaller display focusing on the pioneering women of the Outback who had an even harder time. Often they lived in isolation in very rudimentary accommodation, quite literally in the middle of nowhere. Their menfolk were busy involved with raising cattle or sheep, fixing fences, looking for water, but the women were tied to the home, raising and educating the children alone, and even giving birth on their own. The Hall of Fame was set up in the Old Gaol, so also had plenty of information about prison life in times gone by.

Over the road was the Alice Springs Reptile Centre with over 100 reptiles on display, and even a crocodile. The staff were very friendly and informative, and told us that they operated a call-out service to local residents when they have an unwelcome visitor, a service they carry out for free on behalf of the NT Government. Their most common capture is for the highly venomous western brown, like the one we had seen on the Oodnadatta Track which, like all their captures, were released into the wild in a safe location.

Something we hadn't expected was a hands-on experience. There were about eight visitors and a couple of staff involved, and we had the chance to hold various lizards and eventually a three metre (10ft) olive python. I never thought I would ever hold a snake, certainly not one so large and heavy, but I can now tick that achievement off my list. I can't really say it was a pleasant experience. Pam also had the chance to handle the same creature and it got a little too friendly as its tail crept up her shorts!

It was here that we had the snake we had seen on the Oodnadatta Track identified and also heard about the dangers of Australian snakes. As I have mentioned before, whilst the continent has a high percentage of the most venomous snakes in the world (mulga, taipan, death adder, tiger, red belly etc.), the number of recorded fatalities is only one or two each year. Contrast that with the 30,000 deaths a year in Sri Lanka from cobra bites, and there has to be a good reason for so few fatalities. It seems that whilst the venom of Australian snakes is very toxic, the fangs of these snakes are very short and simply covering exposed skin usually provides adequate protection. The cobra and other venomous snakes around the world have much longer fangs and their attacking bite can penetrate the skin and any layers of clothing, resulting in their venom having a much better chance of entering the blood stream.

Only the day before, we heard of a recent fatality in Darwin. A young and fit rugby player had been coaching some children at a rugby ground when he spotted a western brown snake approaching from nearby scrub. Apparently he didn't want the children put at risk so picked up the snake by the tail and carried it into the scrub to release it. The coaching session finished soon afterwards and he then decided to go for a jog where he was found collapsed by the road. Unbeknown to him, the snake had given him a grazing bite on his leg and going for a jog was the worst thing to do as the vigorous exercise spread the venom round his body. His life support system was switched off when there was no chance of recovery. A salutary tale.

The road train is the lifeblood of the Outback and this is recognised at the Road Transport Museum where there was a large display of the vehicles and a Hall of Fame highlighting key figures in the industry and their role. Next door in an old railway station was a small museum to the Ghan railway, and we spent some time in there – it was inside and cool.

With the medical delay in Sydney and our brief sojourn in New South Wales for the Condo 750 motorsports event, we were well behind the rough schedule I had originally set out for our travels. Australia is effectively divided in two by the Stuart Highway which runs from Darwin in the north, through Alice Springs and south to Port Augusta, and then offers various routes further south to Adelaide, or east into NSW.

However, from this bisecting line, there are only two tarmac roads heading west into WA, one roughly following the north coast via Broome, Port Hedland and Geraldton to Perth, the other heading west from Port Augusta via the Nullabor Plain. In between, it is very difficult to cross the continent to the west, with just the gravel Tanami Track heading north-west to Halls Creek from Alice, and the Gunbarrel Highway/Great Central Highway heading out into the desert from near Uluru. On this route, one ends up at Laverton, and even then it is a long way before one gets to Kalgoorlie and the main populated regions of WA.

I had at one time hoped to use the Outback Highway, also known as the Great Central Highway, but I wasn't convinced our fuel range was sufficient to travel between the few remote fuel stops on the road, and even then it was possible they would only stock diesel rather than petrol.

So it was time to sit down and work out what route we should take, and also decide whether we had enough time to complete a circle of Western Australia and still get back to Sydney in time to stay with our daughter and sell Matilda before heading home. I spent an afternoon with maps and a calculator working out various route options, and, after some head scratching, reckoned that if we missed out the far south-west of Western Australia, we should be able to make it without too much rush. Unfortunately, the area we would miss included the beautiful seaside towns of Esperance and Albany as well as the Margaret Valley wine region, all of which we had heard were well worth the visit. So be it – they will have to wait until the next time.

West MacDonnell Range

Refreshed and with Matilda in fine fettle again, we headed off. Our aim was Uluru and the neighbouring natural wonders.

Whilst most tourists wanting to get to Uluru head south out of Alice Springs down the Stuart Highway to Erldunda and then west along the Lasseter Highway, all of which is now tarmac, we decided to drive along the West MacDonnell Range visiting various gorges as we went, and then head south to visit Kings Canyon and then Uluru. This road is known as the Mereenie Loop, and as it crossed Aboriginal land, we first had to obtain a permit (A$5) from the Visitor Information Centre in Alice.

The MacDonnell's are pierced by several gorges and we stopped at several, walking in from nearby car parks to enjoy their serenity. There were few visitors and all was quiet as we walked into Simpsons Gap, Standley Chasm, Ellery Creek and Big Hole, and the hills around kept the wind away. Some had pools of water that were very still and reflected the colourful surrounding rocks. All in all, it was an enjoyable few hours; we even saw large goanna (monitor lizard).

It was here that we began to have serious problems with flies when out of Matilda. The standard Australian wave to keep them away from the face wasn't enough anymore so we took to wearing a net over our heads for a while. Fortunately, it was a temporary problem, as apart from a day in Uluru when we had the same problem, it was only here that we used our burkhas.

Ormiston Gorge had a small campsite so we stopped for the night. The warden had recently been to France and seen the Tour de France, something we had done the year before starting our Australian adventure. He was also keen to go to the Isle of Man TT motorcycle races, so we had plenty to talk about.

In the morning, we headed off and stopped at Glen Helen Resort, a rather run-down and shabby place, for fuel. Nearby was a viewpoint on a low rise that offered a view over the Finke River, supposedly the oldest river on the planet, and probably 300+ million years old. On our visit, it was dried up and along its course to the east were a series of waterholes, although after heavy rain it can become a fast-flowing torrent that will discharge, eventually, into the north-west of the Lake Eyre basin.

Most of the road was tarmac so we made good progress and turned off to take a look at Gosse Bluff, an ancient impact crater from a meteorite that hit the Earth about 140 million years ago. We had seen the crater from a distant view spot and with the crater being about 5 km (3 miles) in diameter, it was an impressive feature. Inside the jagged, rocky, surround, the floor of the crater was smooth sand and but for the heat, we would have taken a walk round.

We turned right onto Larapinta Drive, which was gravel, until we arrived at Kings Canyon about 160 km (100 miles) distant. The road was the roughest we travelled on during our whole trip and it was very badly corrugated. Poor old Matilda was shaking up and down, the suspension taking the brunt of the torture, but we were similarly all shook up. It mattered not whether we drove slowly or fast, the level of discomfort was much the same, and we just had to put up with it until we reached the tarmac as we drove into Kings Canyon Resort. It was along here that we watched out for a couple of famous road signs that are mentioned in many of the standard guide books. Scrawled onto an old oil drum as one approaches a bend is a sign: *'Lift 'um foot'*, and then soon after another with the inscription: *'Put 'um foot down again'*. Only in Australia!

Kings Canyon itself was further down the road but the resort offered a selection of accommodation options, including a large, rather disorganised, campsite. When we booked a couple of nights in the resort office, we were designated a site only to find someone else parked up there with no intention of moving. Returning to the office, we were directed to another pitch, and as we set up, someone else drove up claiming it was theirs. It took some sorting out but all was well – eventually.

In the morning, we made an early start as we intended taking the walk around Kings Canyon and wanted to take advantage of the cooler temperatures and avoid the midday heat. At the car park, it was clear other people had the same idea as there were several coaches full of tourists, as well as independent travellers such as us. We got talking to George, a Grey Nomad from the Perth area, and did the complete walk with him while his wife wandered off to do some birdwatching.

There were several walking options but we decided on the main Canyon rim walk, which would be about 7 km (4 miles) long, with a steep climb up to the rim edge, about 300 ft above the car park. Immediately, there were great views of the canyon below and the surrounding countryside. The sandstone rock at Kings Canyon is layered red and black, and erosion over millions of years has created rock domes that one can walk amongst. There is a general route to follow, but we had to be careful as the rock levels changed all the time and the surface was a bit loose. While we were there, someone badly twisted their ankle and had trouble getting down and back to the car park. We walked to the rim edge and could see other walkers ahead of us who had been around the edge of the rim and were over the other side. The sides are almost vertical and very impressive.

Approximately halfway round, we had to descend down wooden steps to the canyon floor and there was a woman here who was petrified at the steepness of the flight of steps and needed encouragement from those around her. She made it, albeit rather slowly, and as she reached the valley floor, there was a small round of applause from the gathered crowd. At the canyon floor, the foliage was lush and green; the area is known as the Garden of Eden. We clambered over the rocks to a rock pool in a corner of the canyon, where the water was utterly still. Sadly, the quiet ambiance of the setting was spoilt by the incessant chatter of a party of students. It was then back to the next set of steps and a climb back up to the canyon top.

We completed the walk round the rest of the rim, meandering through more rock domes and outcrops, and after stopping at the rim edge to look down into the canyon again, we descended on a gentle path back to the car park. It was a first class walk; the canyon scenery was rugged and dramatic, and it was certainly one of the top five places we would visit in Australia.

A dingo seen at Kings Canyon, NT

That night, we heard dingoes again and back at the site later in the morning, a rather scruffy dingo could be seen wandering around at the periphery of the site. It was in a poor state, with one limp ear, and it would regularly sit down and howl out. Eventually, it wandered into the bush and was gone.

Uluru

The next day, we drove on towards Uluru, and in the blinding low sun as we drove east, I nearly hit a pack of eight or nine wild camels that were wandering over the road. We headed on to join the Lasseter Highway, and before long stopped at a lay-by with a view south towards Mt Connor.

A wild camel seen near Uluru, NT

The mountain stands out as a mesa in the desert scrub with steep sides and flat top. It is some miles south of the highway and we heard that some people stop here thinking they have reached Uluru, take a photo, and turn around and head back to Alice Springs. Even the maps of the area have a note stating, *'Mt Connor – often mistaken for Uluru'*.

Our companion on the walk around Kings Canyon had given us a tip, because over the road from the parking area was a sandy path that climbed over a dune and a few yards on was a great view of a salt pan. It is worth the look.

Being such an Australian icon, Ayers Rock, now known by its Aboriginal name of Uluru, attracts a huge number of visitors. To minimise their impact on the area, a separate complex called Yulara has been created about 10 km (6 miles) away with all the necessary services, such as shops, petrol station, hotels and a campsite. So now the monolith stands on its own, except for a couple of viewing spots, one for sunrise, the other for sunset.

Uluru, the great Australian icon, formerly known as Ayers Rock

Uluru is an enormous single piece of stone which is known the world over and seems to have a certain mystical attraction that draws one towards it. It is roughly in the centre of the continent and because it is in a remote, arid location, until the advent of modern transport systems, it was fairly difficult to get to. Even now, getting to Uluru is a long flight from one of the major Australian cities, it is a long way from Alice Springs should one choose to head to the region by train, and by road you have to be pretty determined to make the trip.

We heard that Uluru has been likened to the Muslim shrine at Mecca, the Kaaba, to which all Muslims are encouraged to visit during their lifetime. Mecca is in Saudi Arabia, roughly at the centre of Muslim countries, and until recently it too was difficult to get to because of its remoteness and lack of adequate transport facilities.

So just as Muslims should visit Mecca at some stage in their life, so Australians seem to have an innate urge to get to Uluru at least once during their life. In addition, it seems that most international tourists also have an urge to get to Uluru. It was now our turn.

After checking into the campsite, we headed to a display area at the community centre and watched an Aboriginal dancing display, then headed off to watch the sun setting against the rocky outcrop of

Uluru. As the time drew near, a big crowd had collected, but even with a reasonably clear sky, I have to confess I didn't find it very spectacular. Similarly, in the morning we rose early to see the sunrise but that, too, was unimpressive. We drove round to the base of the rock where those with the inclination can climb up the huge edifice, something that is discouraged by the tourist authorities and Aboriginals as it is a sacred place for the latter. Nevertheless, there was a steady trickle of people making the effort; it looked steep and dangerous and we had heard some tragic tales of people stranded on top, blown over the edge or injured, usually seriously, when they have fallen. We decided not to climb Uluru, as the sun was up and the day would become very hot quite soon, and Pam was also adamant that we should respect the Aboriginal sacred place.

Later in the day, we headed out 50 km (30 miles) or so to Kata Tjuta as the Olga stone mounds are now known. These looked much more interesting but we didn't have time to wander through them, so watched the sunset instead. These were much more impressive and the silhouetted rocks outlined against the setting sun looked startlingly beautiful.

In my opinion, the rocky outcrops at Kata Tjuta (formerly known as the Olgas) are far more interesting than nearby Uluru

South on the Stuart Highway

The next day, our long trek to Western Australia began and we headed back to the Stuart Highway and south, intending to get as far as we could. It struck me that most of the traffic on the road was tourist vehicles, caravans, motorhomes and camping trailers and, of course, road trains. Many of the tourist vehicles would have been Grey Nomads venturing north for the Australian winter (it was early May).

We had our only scary driving 'moment' here. We noticed a road train coming the other way, one with four trailers carrying fuel, but as it trundled towards us, the trailers started weaving about, over onto our side of the road, and then back onto the gravelly verge throwing up clouds of dust. The driver obviously caught onto the situation very quickly because he seemed to 'catch it' and the weaving trailers quickly got back in line. We took some deep breaths of relief!

We had driven 640 km (400 miles) yesterday and would do another 680 km (425 miles) today, which included a brief stop at Coober Pedy, a town noted for its opal mining, underground shops and accommodation created from former mine workings. The town even has a *'Public Noodling Centre'*, which sounded a bit risqué, although we didn't investigate.

The area around Coober Pedy is something of a moonscape as the town is surrounded by mounds of spoil from the mining. We could have spent time there visiting a mine and looking at the numerous underground attractions but decided to head off, as on our last trip to Australia, we had visited White Cliffs (NSW) which has similar attractions.

Further south, we also took a brief diversion to Woomera, the base site of a former rocket testing range that extended north and west into the vast desert regions of South Australia. The town was a bit desolate as it is still a military base and there were few people about. There was, however, an open display of rocketry that had been tested there, as well as a Canberra bomber.

Nullabor Plain

We stopped at Port Augusta for the night, which is at the bottom end of the Stuart Highway, and in the morning started our transit west towards Western Australia. Time constraints meant we would miss exploring the Eyre Peninsula so we headed towards Ceduna, taking a short diversion to Streaky Bay. Here we were able to park on the beach to eat our lunch – it was definitely a place to consider a longer visit in the future; the bay was beautiful. The town also looked to be very pleasant and there was a campsite right on the beach.

After our short sojourn in Ceduna, we realised that after our inland travels in recent weeks, we had missed the sight and sounds of the sea and wanted another chance to enjoy the fresh breezes and ozone. We heard there was a pleasant little resort at Fowlers Bay so took side roads and stopped in the caravan site. This was a quiet little fishing community with a friendly couple running the site, café and little shop, and we were glad we took the diversion. The community was dominated by a swathe of tall sand dunes which rise above the community and provided a great walking opportunity. We clambered over the dunes, up, down and up again, over and over again – it was a good and welcome workout with great views over the little town and the ocean. The dunes are gradually creeping towards the current town, having already covered the original small community set up here in the nineteenth century.

It was a Saturday, the day the couple running the site hold a cook up and light their campfire. We all sat round the warm fire and enjoyed good company, good food and drink (again), and the fish was very fresh. I had a long chat with the former manager of Pardoo Cattle Station near Port Hedland, which we would pass in a few weeks' time. Pardoo Station covered 500,000 acres and usually held 7,000 cattle; gigantic by British standards. By comparison, Pam chatted to a chap who was the first to sail single handed around Australia – no mean feat. Yet another great evening. In the morning, he called by and gave Pam a book about his sailing exploits that started in the UK when, at 16 years of age, he sailed across the Atlantic in the company of another 16-year-old.

The next couple of days would be taken up with crossing the Nullabor Plain, a long, boring drive which included the longest length of straight road on the continent at 144 km (90 miles). I had expected the Nullabor Plain to be desert, and whilst it was flat and almost devoid of trees, there was plenty of shrubbery and plants and, at times, turnings to cattle stations. Nullabor means 'no trees', so perhaps their absence was hardly surprising.

As we were approaching Western Australia, where it is forbidden to import fruit, we limited our shopping, and in the evening we cooked up what vegetables we had, freezing the remainder.

The Eyre Highway, as the road is called, is the only sealed road across the south of Australia so it attracts a lot of traffic, especially road trains, and they were running day and night. Inevitably, the road also attracts much tourist traffic, and motorhomes and caravans were on the road aplenty.

Being a busy highway, it is inevitable that occasionally there is a need for the RFDS to land their aircraft to attend road accidents, and to facilitate this every so often the road is identified as a landing strip; it is wider, has aircraft turning circles laid out at each end, and has appropriate signs.

Initially, the road follows a path well inland until it takes a route closer to the Great Australian Bight, the wide, open-curved bay that forms a major part of southern Australia. Near the Nullabor Roadhouse, we took a side track to the Head of Bight Interpretive Centre where, in season, one can spot Southern Right Whales, but sadly we were out of season and it was pouring with rain so we moved on.

Now we could regularly see the coastal waters from the road and we took one side track to park up near the top of the cliffs to take some photos and admire the view. Soon after, we passed into Western Australia, but not before being very thoroughly checked again at a quarantine checkpoint for illegal fruit and vegetables.

By late afternoon, we had stopped briefly in Eucla and then decided to free camp, so pulled into a large lay-by and parked right up the back on our own and well away from the road – it was very quiet except for the occasional rumble from distant road trains on the main highway.

We left in the morning while it was still dark and saw the occasional 'roo and quite a few eagles. We had been recommended to stop at Cocklebiddy Caves where there was a free camp, but the timing was wrong (it was still only 10.00 a.m. and we wanted to keep going), so we headed on to Balladonia, but not before traversing the 144 km (90 miles) of the longest length of straight road in Australia.

There was little more than a roadhouse at Balladonia but it had a small museum adjoining the coffee shop that recorded some of the notable events in the area. I was particularly interested in the Redex Trial, a series of round Australia car rallies that took place in the 1950s and which had passed this way: there were photos and press cuttings and a montage featuring an old rally car.

Balladonia's other claim to fame is the crash landing of a NASA's Skylab in surrounding countryside back in 1979. The museum had samples of the wrecked Skylab panels and other bits and pieces found nearby.

Occasionally we had seen cyclists on the road as a circuit of Australia is a route favoured by some individuals, but along here we came across our first walker, stepping out heading east and pushing a trolley loaded with gear. Mad!

By late afternoon, we had made it to Norseman and decided we would stay a couple of nights so as to take a breather and plan the next few days. We found the town to be very run-down, lots of boarded-up shops and dilapidated properties, the result of the town having run out of gold mining opportunities and everyone moving on to the next rich seam. One benefit was that local property prices were at rock bottom and someone had just bought what was supposedly the cheapest house in Australia for just A$10,000, about £6,250.

Our walk around Norseman brought us to a statue of a horse called Norse which is celebrated locally having given the town its name. Legend has it that Norse discovered the local gold mining potential when it pared the ground and low and behold uncovered a nugget.

From Norseman, we had two choices of route. As mentioned earlier, we needed to be mindful of the need to be back in Sydney in mid-August so we had decided to cut out the south-west corner of Western Australia, which was sad, but we had to be sensible and we couldn't see it all.

So we headed north and over the next few days, we continued to traverse Western Australia, stopping first at Coolgardie, another town with a gold mining past, for coffee. The town had a wide main street with imposing late Victorian buildings lining each side. These had once housed banks and the offices of eight newspapers that were published in the town, but now they were largely empty.

Whilst we were in Coolgardie, we picked up some information about the water supply for the town, and nearby Kalgoorlie, which is supplied by a 530 km (330 mile) pipeline from the Perth suburbs. It wasn't long before we came across the pipeline as it follows the main road for many miles.

The pipeline had been built at the end of the nineteenth century when a regular supply of water was needed for the two towns that were growing with the gold rush. An Irish engineer, Charles Yelverton O'Connor, had recently carried out a major contract to widen the entrance to Fremantle Harbour so the Western Australian Government appointed him to design and build the pipeline.

It was a huge task; 60,000 lengths of pipe would be required, dams and several pumping stations needed to be built. It was an incredible feat of engineering that would take five years to complete, but O'Connor was subjected to much criticism and accusations of financial shenanigans, and committed suicide before the project could be finished. The pipeline continues to be in use today with much of the water it supplies now being used in agriculture.

For several weeks, we'd had a problem with Matilda that I had tried to fix a few times but which still persisted. The adjustment on the wardrobe door needed a professional touch and as we drove through Nungarin, I noticed a kitchen fitting workshop alongside the only shop in the town. I checked inside but they couldn't help so referred me to Ray, who lived nearby, and was the local handyman. Ray proved to be an absolute star, and very helpful. While he got his tools out and spent about half an hour adjusting the door, his wife showed Pam around their home which they were renovating. Needless to say, Ray wouldn't take anything for his efforts – he told me he was glad to have someone to chat to, other than his wife!

My motor racing interest was engaged again when we got to Dowerin and in a second-hand bookshop I learned of local motorcycle road races that used to take place in the region before World War II. I bought a couple of books on the subject and we had to tear ourselves away when the owner joined his wife and wouldn't stop talking. The track in Dowerin was long gone; however, we did learn that the next town, Goomalling, had held motorcycle races round the town, so we headed there for a look.

Goomalling had a small campsite so we checked in there and then took a drive round the streets following the circuit plan we had previously picked up. As the town was set out on a grid pattern, the route wasn't too interesting – all 90° left and right turns and straights. The campsite though was just about the cheapest 'proper' site we had found and was supported financially by the local council to help attract visitors to the area.

Part 6

* Reaching the west coast
* Geraldton
* Shark Bay
* Coral Bay
* Into the Pilbara
* Karijini National Park
* Busy roads
* Broome
* The Kimberley
* The Bungle Bungles

Reaching the west coast

We didn't want to go into Perth or its suburbs, so in the morning we cut across country via Toodyay, then onto a lovely road through a military training area to Bindoon where we took a breather at a great coffee shop and bakery. We found the place by chance; it was on the main road north out of Perth so there was plenty of passing traffic, but time and again over the next few weeks people mentioned the coffee stop and it was clearly a very popular stopping place. The staff were friendly, the cakes we bought were tasty and we must have been lucky to come upon it.

Then it was on towards the Indian Ocean, where we thought we would try something different and stop at the Gravity Discovery Centre. This was something of a modern Science Museum with lots of displays and hands-on experiments that could be carried out, all targeting basic physics principles such as gravity, light, sound, mass, magnetism and more. Outside the main building were other exhibits including a leaning tower, but it was drizzling so we gave it a miss. It was a fascinating place and a pleasant diversion from the travelling and natural scenery we had been lapping up during our journey.

We were ready to see the sea again so headed for Sea Bird where there was supposed to be a campsite; however, it was a residential site, and as we wandered around the community, we met up with another couple we'd seen at Gravity and who were also looking for somewhere to stop in their motorhome.

Vanessa and Greg were from Kempsey, NSW, about an hour's drive north of Sydney, and were on an extended trip in a large Winnebago motorhome towing a small 4x4. We had spoken to them briefly at the Gravity Centre and, as we were both looking to stop for the night, parked up in a car park overlooking the ocean and yarned away while we had a drink or two and watched the sun set.

The next day, we followed the almost new Indian Ocean Drive to Lancelin and Wedge Island where we planned to take a walk amongst the shacks that are hidden away in the sand dunes. Alas, I slipped in a bit of mud and crashed onto my backside and was filthy. The camera was covered in sand and mud and took a while to clean up. No serious damage was done, except to my pride, so we decided to move on to the Pinnacles, a natural wonder and well-known tourist destination nearby. Here we found a large Visitor Information Centre, car park and hundreds of tourists who, like us, wanted to see the famous rock pinnacles.

The rocks in the Pinnacles National Park, north of Perth, are an unusual and visually interesting scene

The pinnacles from which the area takes its name are limestone outcrops worn down over aeons to form several thousand small rock towers up to 20ft high, and all within an area confined to about 350 acres. We could drive around them and walk amongst them and they proved to be fascinating, but eerie at the same time. A quite remarkable natural feature.

For the night, we headed on to Cervantes and stopped for a couple of days to catch up with the normal domestics. The small town was very quiet with only one shop and a pub, where we had a great fish meal, but our second day there was marred by more or less continuous rain and we were confined to Matilda all day; rare over here, but common enough when we travel at home.

Nearby was Lake Thetis, a saline water feature and one of the few places on Earth to see marine stromatolites. These are also known as living fossils as, whilst they look like rocky lumps or large cowpats, they are some of the oldest life forms on the planet, at about 3,500 years old. There was a walkway around the lake and information boards so we took a stroll round and examined the stromatolites from above. Whilst they are nothing to look at, we felt privileged to be amongst such ancient organisms.

Jurien Bay was our next stop, mainly for supplies and one of the best fish lunches ever, before we moved on again following the coast road and investigating a couple of beach stopovers before settling on Cliff Head. This was a spread out beach spot with several RV units parked up amongst the trees and along the line of dunes. We set up right on the beach; the water was about 10ft away, with the only problem being a lot of seaweed. But it wasn't long before we got out the chairs, poured the chilled wine and whiled away an hour or so watching the sun go down as the sea lapped against the foreshore in front of us. A magical time and it was hard to see why we would ever want to go home.

In the morning at Dongara, a modest community with large fig trees providing welcome shade along the main street, we stopped at a beachside café and bumped into Vanessa and Greg again, and after swapping notes with them, headed on to Geraldton, a major port and the largest town in the region.

Geraldton

It was time for some serious repairs and maintenance, so we took full advantage of a few days here and had my computer hard disk replaced, and an electrician had a look at our sidelights which had been working intermittently for some time. We also had the main door rebuilt – it wasn't closing properly. It sounds like a lot of work, but it was wear and tear brought about by our hectic travels and the nature of the terrain we were investigating, especially the corrugated roads, and was to be expected.

Our new friends, Vanessa and Greg, turned up at the campsite and we spent a very relaxed and enjoyable day touring the main sites of Geraldton in the car they were towing behind their motorhome. One, a memorial to the loss of *HMAS Sydney*, was especially interesting and poignant at the same time. The cruiser was sunk by a German warship posing as a merchant vessel on 19th November 1941 with the loss of 645 men, the whole crew. The German ship, the *Kormoran*, was also lost in the encounter, with a further loss of nearly 400 men, although some of the crew survived and managed to reach safety on the mainland.

The loss of the battleship had a considerable effect on the Australian psyche, never more so than in Geraldton which the *HMAS Sydney* visited a few days before being sunk. Despite numerous searches, wreckage of the ship was not found until March 2008 when some closure of the loss was possible.

The next couple of weeks would turn out to be some of the most scenic and relaxing travel we did on our jaunt round Australia. We knew we would be heading into territory where the communities were smaller and more infrequent, and even if the main road (Route 1) and some roads around the towns were sealed, anything else was gravel.

North of Geraldton, we took in the Kalbarri loop but did not stop other than for a photo. Kalbarri is a very picturesque town at the mouth of the Murchison River and is surrounded by a national park. It is popular for water sports and bushwalking, and we put it down for another visit at some time in the future.

Once back on Route 1, we made straight for the Overlander Roadhouse for a breather and fuel. We were now on the north-west edge of Australia, about as far as we could get from our family in Sydney. If one looks at a map, there are two fingers of land pointing north from the main landmass and we would visit them next.

Shark Bay

Driving west from the Overland Roadhouse, we entered the Shark Bay World Heritage Area, an area full of history, wonderful natural features as well as fauna and flora, and, maybe, an opportunity to feed dolphins.

The main body of water in and around the two peninsulas is Shark Bay, a very shallow and saline bay, but one that attracts a wide range of marine life. The first finger of land is the Peron Peninsula with the main town of the area, Denham, on the west side. It faces the other finger of land, Useless Loop, a remote area that I would have liked to visit had we the time. On Useless Loop, so called after a French explorer who sailed by and saw no purpose for the land, there is a small community at a salt extraction plant and its vast lagoons.

Atop Useless Loop lies a slither of land named Dirk Hartog Island after the Dutch merchantman who was the first European to visit Australia in 1616, long before James Cook. Hartog's was a short visit as he was heading for Batavia in Indonesia, but he left behind a pewter plate with a suitable inscription that he left affixed to a post. Amazingly, another Dutchman came to the same spot 80 years later, found the plate and removed it, and left behind his own. They are now museum pieces and treasured artefacts.

Heading into the area, we first stopped at Hamelin Pool to look at more stromatolites. Here there was another boardwalk over the edge of the water where the stromatolites grow. They were covered in sea water when we visited and extended over an area about the size of a football pitch. Like the others we had seen, they looked like rocky outcrops. These had a reddish tinge to them and somehow a fascinating charm.

We were at the southern end of the bay and the low coastline stretched out before us to the east and west. The water was still and the weather was bright, and whilst it was tempting to stay at the nearby campsite, we felt we should move on to a much more interesting attraction.

A short drive took us to Denham where we found the caravan park, the most westerly in Australia, to be chock-a-block full and we had to camp on some open ground at the back of the site, not a problem as we didn't plan to stay very long.

It was an early start in the morning and in the dark we headed a few kilometres to Monkey Mia so as to catch the dolphin feeding that takes place on the beach each day. It is thought that bottlenose dolphins have been coming to the beach for more than 40 years originally attracted by fishing boats and the fishermen who fed them. Gradually, news of the phenomenon spread and Monkey Mia started to attract visitors to see the spectacle and now there is a hotel complex, a wildlife centre – and a large car park.

Gradually, a crowd of about 40 people gathered on the beach and we were addressed by wildlife wardens about how the feeding takes place and how we might be able to be involved. The whole interaction with the dolphins is carefully controlled and it was likely that three or four dolphins would be visiting the beach and would return a couple of times more during the morning. We all lined up in the water standing in about a foot of warm water, and, after a few minutes, the first dolphins appeared and swam around us. Then, when they seemed settled, they were fed some fish by the wardens, and then one or two of the tourists.

Dolphins come for hand feeding at Monkey Mia, Shark Bay, WA

After 20 minutes or so, the dolphins swam away and many of the tourists dispersed as well and those who were left were told it might be an hour or two before the dolphins returned. We wanted to make sure we were present for the return so wandered up and down the beach for a while, and sure enough the dolphins reappeared and the scene was repeated with fewer people present.

After this display, we went off for some coffee and returned to the beach a third time and the dolphins were there once more, with only about a dozen tourists. This time we got to feed them and were able to hold out a piece of fish at water level a couple of times and let the dolphins take them from our hands. The wardens had names for each of the dolphins, and Pam had fed Piccolo, whilst I fed one called Nicky.

It was a very special experience, one we had hoped to enjoy on our trip and matched the time we had a similar interaction with cheetahs when on a holiday in Namibia.

While we were hanging around, I booked an evening boat trip in Shark Bay, and mid-afternoon we boarded a catamaran, and with just a few other guests, we headed off across the bay. It was very enjoyable sitting with a beer watching the sun go down, and the bonus was that we saw a fabulous array of marine creatures as well. We saw more dolphins, a green turtle, a sea eagle, dugong (also known as a sea cow), an eagle manta ray, a loggerhead turtle, and a tiger shark – quite an amazing bag. We'd had a terrific day and it was dark as we drove back to the campsite and crashed out for the night.

We had a leisurely wander round town the next morning, taking a look at the Visitor Information Centre and the jetty where a small fleet of fishing boats were in attendance. The town has a long promenade so we walked the length and sat reading while the sea lapped against the nearby shore. I loved the gentle laid-back ambiance of the place and it really was the sort of place I would want to live if I ever got the chance to emigrate to Australia permanently.

An odd incident occurred as we headed back to the Overland Roadhouse. While we were in Denham, we had seen information about a great view spot a few miles down the road and thought we would take a look and maybe have some lunch there. The centre staff told us the gravel road leading up to the view spot had been closed because it was rain damaged, but while we were talking she was told it had now been re-opened.

So off we went, and after half an hour's drive, we found the turning off the main road – with a closed sign board on it. However, the road looked fine, we had heard it was open, and anyway, we had a four-wheel drive vehicle so could cope should the road be damaged. So we headed up the road, and about two miles later we came to the view spot and it offered great views of the ocean and the surrounding countryside.

There were several tracks leading along the cliff top so we took one and found an even better spot and decided to have our lunch there, as it happens, watching a sea eagle patrolling up and down the beaches either side of the headland we were now on.

One of several white-breasted sea eagles we saw. This one was on the Mary River, NT

We were munching away when all of a sudden, a 4x4 came zooming round the corner, pulled up and a warden got out and strode over to Matilda.

"You can't park here. Didn't you see the 'Road Closed' sign?"

To be honest, I was rather taken aback. His tone and body language were quite unnecessary. A proper jobsworth.

"Why not? We were told in Denham that this road has just been re-opened. We saw the sign, and, as the road looks in good condition, decided nobody had had the time to remove it."

"That's not the point. You can be fined A$1,000 a wheel for driving on a closed road, and have to pay for any damage. That would be A$6,000 for your vehicle."

"Yes, I know that. But there's no damage and we have been told by the Information Centre that the road was open. Who should we believe? Are you saying the road is still closed?"

"You drove past a 'Road Closed' sign and that can lead to a big fine. I suggest you don't do it again". And with that, he turned and walked back to his 4x4 and drove away.

It reminded me of the time we had driven down the unsealed Darling River Run between Bourke and Wilcannia in New South Wales during our last trip to Australia. We were in a hire car and I knew there had been rain in previous days and some roads were closed, as mentioned in my comments about meeting some sheep shearers in Tilpa. I checked with the police who confirmed the road was open and it was them who told me about the potential for being fined for travelling on closed roads. You can also be lumbered with the cost of repairing the road as well.

In reality the road was still flooded; we saw signs of cars turning round after travelling along for a mile or two and clearly deciding it was not for them, but we also came across a motorhome coming the other way, and one or two other cars and 4x4s. In our little two-wheel drive car, it was a challenging drive; there were several 100m (110 yards) sections that were flooded and a lot of mud. There was so much mud that when we got to Wilcannia and reached some tarmac, I went to turn the wheel and the build-up of mud in the wheel arches prevented the wheels turning! I had to get out and clear some away.

Back in WA, we debated whether to stay on but thought we would head off and stopped at Eagle Bluff. There were other travellers already there but with plenty of space we soon found our own spot right down by the beach. We sat out and, guess what? We enjoyed yet another sunset while supping some alcohol. Life can be really tough in Australia!

In the morning, we had breakfast sitting on the beach and then packed up ready to go. I started up Matilda and .... she was stuck! The wheels were spinning in the sand and gradually digging a hole for themselves. We spent about an hour trying to get moving and tried all the usual tricks. We gathered brush and wood and pushed it under the wheels. We added as many stones as we could find and I tried jacking Matilda up so as to get more grippy materials under the wheels. She would not budge.

By now there was nobody around, and after a council of war, we had to admit defeat and get outside help. We prepared for a walk out to the tarmac road into Denham, probably about 5 km (3 miles) away, and headed off. By chance, we came across a young couple camped with a 4x4 further along the beach and the guy offered to have a look and help us, or even try towing us out with his own vehicle. We walked back and he looked around, while I started Matilda up and tried to get out again.

No luck, but our new friend, Brodie, noticed the front wheels weren't turning. Was 4x4 engaged? I thought it was, but clearly it wasn't. Oops! So I got 4x4 engaged, and low and behold we drove out without any problems, but rather embarrassed! Doh! I have no doubt he now tells all his mates about how he met a couple of old Poms who were stuck in the sand and couldn't get out because they didn't engage four-wheel drive. We drove sheepishly away!

It was the only time we got stuck while in Australia, although we did get stuck in a hired motorhome in New Zealand during our time there before getting to Australia. We spent six weeks driving round the North and South Islands and were in the south-east corner of the North Island. On a pleasant Sunday afternoon, we were driving in a rural area to visit *Tetaumatawhakatangihangakoauaotamateaureha eaturipukapihimaungah*, the longest place name in the world, and a small village nearby, Wimbledon.

Wimbledon was really not much more than a crossroads and a few houses spread around the local area, but there was a dilapidated school building and, behind it, a tennis court. I pulled over onto the grass verge and immediately the nearside wheels sank into the soft grass. There was no way we could drive out, despite trying: we were well and truly stuck. While Pam, the tennis fan, had a look at the tennis court, I tried to get help at a couple of local houses, but couldn't raise anybody.

Then a lorry came round the corner, an almost brand new fuel tanker and I waved the driver down and explained the problem. At first, he was reluctant to help, claiming, "It's a new vehicle, my insurance doesn't cover me for towing. I have a full fuel load on board," but eventually he decided he needed to try out the new tow rope he had on board. We hooked up the rope, and in moments we were back on the road.

It was then that he told us that he hadn't done this particular trip on a Sunday before, and, if he hadn't helped us, he couldn't see us getting any help until the morning. How lucky were we? I slipped a bottle of wine into the glovebox of his lorry before he drove away. Thanks, mate. We did the same for our new friend, Brodie.

Back in Australia, we headed off back to the Overlander Roadhouse for fuel, then continued our journey north and arrived in Carnarvon by mid-afternoon. In the morning, we went into town and had a walk along a one-mile jetty that was very blowy but refreshing. The region is the centre of a lot of fruit and vegetable growing and the roadsides were littered with farmer's stalls, so it was a good chance to stock up with cheap produce. We also tried some specialist ice cream; I had one with an apple pie flavour, and Pam had a mango and chocolate lolly. Lovely.

*This sign in WA provides adequate warning of shortages
ahead on Route 1, the main road across northern Australia*

We were driving on Route 1, the main road that would lead us across the top of Australia, and the main road around the continent. However, as we left Carnarvon, we were reminded of the potential remoteness of so much of Australia by a road sign that warned, *'Limited water for next 632 km. Obtain supplies in Carnarvon'* – that's 400 miles! Imagine driving that distance in the UK, or any other developed nation, without the potential for stocking up with water. Australia is a very different place. We were alright as the water tank on Matilda had 110 litres, and we always had a stock of bottled water as well.

Soon after leaving Carnarvon, we diverted off the main road to Point Quobba. Before coming to Australia, I had been following the blog of an Australian couple doing more or less what we were doing, and they had been to Quobba and it seemed a great place. There was wild camping beside the sea, lovely bays and beaches, and supposedly great swimming and snorkelling. We parked up and took a good walk round and headed for the real attraction, a series of blowholes where the sea water shoots about 30 feet into the air through several rock holes.

We watched for ages; it was a great spectacle, and once we tired of it, we wandered back to the camping area but decided it was not for us. It was a very popular spot and rather crowded and we decided to head on and eventually stopped at another wild camp spot on the road heading for Exmouth. It was just a lay-by and was quiet and pleasant enough for the night, and we would have a short drive to our next destination, Coral Bay, in the morning.

Coral Bay

Coral Bay was as idyllic as its name suggests. To one side of a wide sandy beach was a caravan site, hotel, a few shops, and that's about it. Numerous people, on hearing we would be travelling in this region of WA, had recommended Coral Bay – and with good reason. There was a laid-back atmosphere, the sky was blue, the sea was warm and a short swim from the beach was Ningaloo Reef.

Once installed in the caravan park, we took a wander round and soon it was off with the sandals and a long walk along the shoreline. We swam too with our snorkels, and less than 100 yards from the beach was the reef just a few feet below us with colourful fish swimming round and all manner of coral. We supped beers in the hotel bar and had a meal in one of the small restaurants (fish, of course) and had a couple of days break from the hectic driving schedule we were on. The whole place was magical.

But, once again, we were reminded of the hidden dangers that lurk in Australia for the unwary. We had heard of a couple with three children who were camping at a remote beach about 80 km (50 miles) north of Coral Bay, on the Exmouth Peninsula. The two adults had gone swimming and had never returned, their children eventually raising the alarm. Extensive searches had not found them and we would eventually learn that one body was recovered many weeks later. We never heard about the other. The general consensus was that while swimming they had encountered a smack of Irukandji, a tiny, highly-venomous jellyfish, and maybe one of them had been badly stung and the other had come to the rescue and been similarly stung.

Into the Pilbara

It would have been nice to head for Exmouth but time constraints meant we had to work our way back towards the main route as we planned to head inland into the Pilbara region, the Hamersley Ranges and the main town. Tom Price, an odd name for a town, was somewhere that was totally different to anything we had encountered previously in Australia.

Tom Price is a mining town, named after an American mining engineer who was responsible for convincing the mining companies to come to the area. It is a modern town with all the usual facilities which we found to be soulless with almost everything covered in red dust from the nearby iron ore mine.

The mine is the main attraction and we booked a trip, and along with about 50 other people, we took a coach out of town to the mine. Unless one has experience of an opencast mine, it is difficult to visualise the immensity of the whole operation. The trucks are huge, the tyres alone are about 12 ft high, they carry huge loads of ore to the plant which is itself vast with conveyors and grinders, and gigantic heaps of spoil and ore. The mine runs 24/7 and there is a steady stream of trains pulling long lines of ore wagons into the base of the plant and a continuous loading procedure sees them drive slowly through, exiting fully loaded ready to head off to the coast, at Port Hedland. Unsurprisingly, everything is plastered in red dust from the ore.

The coach pulled up at an old working, a huge hole in the ground, maybe 200ft deep, whilst across on the other side, explosives were being put in place and fresh rock blasted away. Nearby, huge trucks ran backwards and forwards from another area of the mine. A massive and impressive operation that, we were told, is largely managed from a headquarters in Perth 1,500 km (950 miles) away. Transponders tell the managers in Perth where all the equipment is and, via radio, they can direct trucks and trains to any particular location.

Karijini National Park

By contrast with dusty Tom Price, our next port of call was a stunning national park that had been recommended by many people as a 'must do'. Karijini National Park wasn't too far away. We paid our A$11 at the honesty box at the entrance, and after stopping to reduce the tyre pressures, headed along quite rough gravel tracks to start looking at some of the dramatic gorges that carve up the landscape in the area.

The park is bisected by two deep gorges. We visited Weano Gorge first, travelling along several kilometres of deep red dusty tracks to get to a lookout from where we could see the dribble of water in the river down below and, further away, a trickle of water falling over a ledge and splashing down layers of rock strata. It was stunning and would have been much more so had there been more water. A pity.

A black-flanked wallaby seen in Karijini National Park

Walking back to Matilda, we heard a rustling in the bush near the track. Thinking the worst, maybe a slithery thing, we hesitated to approach but curiosity got the better of us, and low and behold a little wallaby was munching on the bush, totally oblivious to us. We stood no more than 10ft away and watched the black-flanked rock wallaby have his fill. It was a super few minutes. We drove round to take a look at Knox Gorge and then went to the Eco Resort to camp for the night.

The next day, we headed for Dale Gorge, a more popular part of the park, and once parked we walked over to the viewpoint that overlooks Circular Pool and down the gorge. Before us, however, a drama was unfolding. It was clear from the expression of people standing around at the viewpoint that something worrying was happening. Looking down to Circular Pool, an almost perfectly round pool into which a stream discharges from the cliff tops next to the view spot, was a group of people gathered around someone laid out on the ground and covered by a space blanket.

"Is something going on?" I asked someone.

"Yes. A guy just jumped off the cliff top into the pool and it looks like he is seriously injured," came the reply.

"Why did he jump?"

"No idea. I think he is a tourist from Eastern Europe and this chap," he pointed at someone standing nearby and looking very concerned, "brought him here from Tom Price to show him round the park."

Further information became apparent over the next few minutes and they revealed he had decided to jump into the pool from near the view point and had landed heavily in the water, nearly hitting some people swimming there. It was thought he had serious internal injuries and maybe spinal damage. It was all very serious and the park medical staff had been called, as well as medics from Tom Price.

There seemed little we could do so we decided to move on and walked around a couple of other view spots providing spectacular views of the gorge and then decided to descend to the base of the gorge via a set of steps. The steps led us to a rock pool where there were several people swimming, but we had heard that another pool further along the gorge was a better spot. We headed off along an uneven path, and after about ten minutes came to Fern Pool alongside which was a small diving platform and more people swimming.

Pam enjoys a refreshing swim in Fern Pool in beautiful Karijini National Park, WA

We hadn't brought our swimmers, but decided we weren't going to go back up to the top to get them, so stripped off to our undies and took the plunge. The water was best described as fresh, not really cold, but not warm either; it was certainly very refreshing. We swam over to the other side of the pool where a 10ft waterfall discharged water into the pool, and we had a good swim round. We dried ourselves off as best we could and headed back to the top and on to Matilda.

After sorting ourselves out, we headed on to the local campground to stay the night and I used the compressor to pump up the tyres again to normal pressure as we would be back on tarmac roads soon after we left the next day.

In the morning, I went to start Matilda, but her battery was flat. Who failed to use the tyre compressor without the engine running so as to keep the battery topped up? Me! Doh!

Off I went to find someone to jump start us and met up with a young couple on a nearby pitch who willingly drove over to give us a hand. Chatting with them, we found out more about the incident yesterday as they had been closely involved. Lisa and Adam had been in the gorge walking to Circular Pool to have a swim. Near the pool, they heard a man shout out from the top, "How deep is the water?" Some people already swimming in the pool shouted out that it was fairly shallow, but he took no notice and jumped off the top, about 100ft above the pool.

He nearly hit those already in the water and was clearly injured and had to be rescued by those present. It so happened that Lisa was a nurse and it was a space blanket from her first aid kit that we had seen. She told us that once medical help arrived, the injured man was strapped to a stretcher and it had taken 20 people nearly five hours to haul him up the side of the gorge to an ambulance.

The incident had happened at about 10.00 a.m. the previous morning and Adam told us that the chap had been 'rather the worse for wear' (drunk!) and the guy we had seen at the top looking very concerned was his mate who thought he was dead.

We learned much later that the injured man had been taken to Port Hedland where his injuries were found to be not as serious as first thought: a very lucky guy who could so easily have been killed or very seriously injured. It was hard to have any sympathy for him.

It wasn't long before we were back on the main road, first east to join the Northern Highway from Newman, and then north where we stopped at Auski Roadhouse. This had huge parking areas for the numerous road trains that were on the highway and I took the opportunity to take a look at some of them. There were also several opportunist kites wheeling around hoping for some food scraps and I managed to catch one sitting on our bull bar investigating the fly cemetery on the front of Matilda.

This whistling kite took a keen interesting in the fly cemetery on the front of Matilda at Auski Roadhouse, WA

Busy roads

It was over 240 km (150 miles) to Port Hedland and the road was incredibly busy. The whole region, from Newman in the south up to the coast, has numerous mines, and these generated most of the traffic. Empty four-trailered road trains passed us going south every 90 seconds or so, and we were driving north in the company of more road trains loaded with ore. Most had four trailers, which meant they probably had almost 100 wheels, but would have been no longer than 53 metres (58 yards), the legal maximum. In the UK, the maximum length for most lorries is 17 metres, so these Australian juggernauts are more than three times longer. In addition, there were other vehicles loaded with mining equipment, other more routine traffic and people like ourselves. In one lay-by were three low-loaders, each carrying massive pieces of mining infrastructure. They were accompanied by escort vehicles and were resting up before moving on, as once on the road it would be completely blocked to other traffic unless it was prepared to go a bit agricultural and hack through the roadside bush.

Port Hedland was our target for the day, a town based around the port where huge mounds of iron ore are loaded onto ships and taken away, the majority to China. There was no charm to the town; it was dominated by the road trains and railway bringing in the raw material, and the infrastructure needed to load the ships. We found a small park and watched as the huge ore carriers came into the dock, a scene backed by more ore carriers waiting in the roads offshore.

Fortunately, the campsite was outside town, alongside a creek, and was fairly pleasant so we stayed a couple of nights before heading on.

Traffic was busy as we were leaving Port Hedland but soon thinned out as we cleared the built-up area and the surrounding industrial activities. The journey to Broome was about 640 km (400 miles) but there is almost nothing in between except a couple of roadhouses and turnings to mines and distant cattle stations.

We passed the entrance to Pardoo Station (I had met the former station manager at a campfire gathering some weeks ago) and stopped at Pardoo Roadhouse for a breather. It was a sobering thought that there is almost nothing to the south of the road for the next few hundred miles as the Great Sandy Desert stretches about 1,600 km (1,000 miles) west and south with completely empty grid squares on the map. The road we were on is the only tarmac road across the north of Australia, and, to the south, one would have to travel to the Nullabor Plain before finding another one. In this day and age, it is hard to imagine such a lack of proper highways in a westernised country, but it again highlights how remote some areas of Australia remain.

Along here we also came across four gigantic mining trucks being moved on low-loaders towards Port Hedland. They were in convoy with attendant support vehicles on a track joining the main road. We stopped to watch them turn out onto the main highway completely blocking both sides.

Numerous people had told us of two campsites worth a visit along this road and we turned off towards the coast down a sandy track to Eighty Mile Beach. We knew of the rain that had caused problems round here a week or two previously and the track was in quite a state but it led to a large camp complex sheltered from the sea by a low sand dune. It was a big site and work was in progress to enlarge it, and most people staying there were set up for long-term stays to go fishing. We stayed two nights, enjoying a long walk on the smooth sandy beach and an evening BBQ organised by the camp attended by about 100 people.

On leaving, we stopped at Sandfire Roadhouse, the last before the long run towards Broome, and spent an age queueing for fuel. Like other roadhouses we had visited, the number of pumps didn't match the level of traffic wanting to use them, and many of them had had little investment in new pumps and storage tanks for a number of years. Here there was a queue of several RVs, as well as ordinary cars, and progress was slow, especially as drivers had to pay for fuel before driving off to enable access to the pump. This is to prevent drive offs, where people drive away without paying for their fuel.

We had been used to seeing roadkill along the verges, but in this area kangaroo carcases were very frequent and we counted 17 in one 5 km (3 miles) stretch. There were occasional cattle, emu and wallaby carcases too, adding to the horrendous toll, but one that was impossible to avoid.

A second campsite recommendation along this road was Barn Hill Outstation where there was another great stop down a sandy track towards the coast. This site was much more rustic than other sites we had stayed at and everyone was very friendly and social. Most campsites we stayed at had modern amenity blocks with hot and cold water, tiled toilet facilities, and so on. Here the toilet block had corrugated iron sides, most WCs and showers had no roof over them, and generally the whole place was very basic. We noticed a sign at the toilet block asking that the lid of the WCs be put back in place after use to stop frogs getting in, but there were usually a couple under the rim and also on the walls.

"Are the frogs common in this part of the world?" I asked our neighbour.

"Oh, don't worry about them, they're no problem. What you have to watch out for are the western browns that slither out of the bushes at night. They like the frogs." After that, we made sure to use the loo in the van at night until we got to Broome!

But the snakes weren't the only creatures keen to feed on frogs. One morning, I noticed a couple of people standing under a tree, one with a camera, the other with binoculars. They were looking at something in the tree and I enquired and found out it was a frog eating owl, but initially I couldn't see it. It was so well camouflaged that it looked like a broken off branch.

Once again, most people were staying for several months and many had tinnies (small aluminium boats with outboard motors) and would go out fishing whenever they could. Catches were usually good and too much for the fisherman's own use so we found ourselves inundated with gifts of fish fillets that we froze until our small freezer was chock-a-block. But it kept us supplied for many days.

There was a great beach here with spectacular rock formations and we took some walks and had a very refreshing swim in the sea. There was also a BBQ evening and once again we enjoyed some good yarning with people from various places around Australia.

Broome

We moved on to Broome, a large regional centre and popular tourist destination, and planned to stay several days so it gave us a chance to have a good look round. There are a couple of places in Australia with open-air cinemas and Broome is one of them so we thought we should try the experience. Our seat was actually under cover, but the first few rows were open to the elements, as was the screen. It was a nice warm evening and we enjoyed watching *The Great Gatsby*. However, we didn't know the cinema was in direct line with the end of Broome's airport runway and the film was interrupted three times as airliners took off and drowned out the sound as they flew right over, appearing from over the screen as they climbed away! A bit different to our local Odeon.

We'd been in Broome for a couple of days when we heard of something called the Horizontal Waterfalls and trips one could book to see them. This was to become our one great regret of the whole trip as they are amazing and we had to miss them.

The falls are a unique natural phenomenon described by Sir David Attenborough as *"one of the greatest natural wonders in the world".* Whilst they are called waterfalls, the phenomenon is actually a very strong tidal current that passes through two narrow coastal gorges creating massive banks of water through which powerful boats are driven. The amazing wall of water occurs again when the tide goes out.

Unfortunately, the trips by sea plane out to the falls and riding in the boats get very booked up, and the phenomenon is best at certain times in the moon's tidal phases. Sadly, we would have had to hang around in Broome for another ten days before we could get on a trip so reluctantly had to give it a miss.

Another natural spectacle in Broome is the Staircase to the Moon, best viewed from Cable Beach. When the tides are low, the rising full moon is reflected on mudflats to create an optical illusion of a stairway rising toward the moon. Conditions weren't perfect when we were there but the sight was nevertheless spectacular and there was a great atmosphere with many tourists waiting for the moment.

We got chatting to three couples who were in Broome after coming unstuck on the Canning Stock Route, the granddaddy of the 4x4 desert trails. The Canning Stock Route, or CSR as it is more often referred to, is a 2,000 km (1,250 miles) long former stock route from the Kimberley Range across the Great Sandy Desert, the Gibson Desert, the Little Sandy Desert and other more remote areas to eventually finish at Wiluna, itself a long way from anywhere. It is only tackled by well-prepared groups that have to be self-sufficient for up to a month, the usual travelling time.

Our new acquaintances had been planning their trip for some time and had driven up from Brisbane to drive the CSR and had only driven 90 km (55 miles) when the whole rear suspension of one of their Toyota Land Cruisers had collapsed. They couldn't repair it themselves but as they were still relatively close to civilisation, they were able to organise a recovery and were very lucky not to have had to abandon the vehicle in the middle of the desert. Australia has a habit of biting back, and this was a typical example.

Broome was a pleasant town and had numerous pearl shops, this being the centre of Australia's pearling industry. We decided to go and take a look at one of the pearl farms and headed up the Cape Leveque road before turning off to Willie Creek on some nice sandy tracks through dunes and scrubland. The trip included a boat trip to the pearl beds and an interesting presentation on the industry.

Swimming in the sea can be a hazardous pastime,
especially in WA where this sign was seen

Just as Europe has a problem with boat people arriving from North Africa seeking a better life, so the problem in Australia was creating a lot of news while we were there. Almost daily there seemed to be news of another boatload of people, most from impoverished backgrounds in war-torn countries, hoping to make it to Australia via Indonesia for a better life. In answer to the problem, the Government had declared that no illegal immigrants will ever be allowed to reside in Australia and would have to make their life, if they settle, in the offshore territories of Papua New Guinea or Nauru.

During our time in Australia, we had met numerous Grey Nomads who had sold their business and house to take to the road full-time in their rig, whether it was a motorhome or caravan. It was here in Broome that we learned of the risks that such a dramatic life change can create. A couple on an adjacent pitch were in dire straits as she couldn't drive and he had become seriously ill needing regular hospital treatment, we suspected with cancer. They were stuck as they couldn't move on, had no home to get back to and faced an uncertain future. Other sites seemed to have people in comparable circumstances, often widows having to see out their days in much reduced circumstances and unable to move on.

By contrast, we had met other Grey Nomads who had been on the road for ages; the longest we heard of was 13 years, this particular couple being on their third caravan. However, they had retained a base which was either let out to provide some additional income, or was there to return to when necessary.

We stayed a few days in Broome and relaxed, just pottering about, something we had found was necessary, as much as a break from the driving. But the need to keep going was ever present as well as the prospect of interesting experiences, so the time came to pack up yet again and hit the road.

The Kimberley

Broadly we were heading east now, through the Kimberley and eventually to Darwin 1,920 km (1,200 miles) away. Our first stop would be Derby, a small town on King Sound and at the start of another great Outback track, the Gibb River Road. The GRR, as it is commonly referred to, is about 770 km (480 miles) long and cuts through the heart of the Kimberley region. There are several side trips that can be tackled in the right vehicle, the Mitchell Falls, Windjana Gorge and Tunnel Creek being the most popular. For the adventurous driver, there is another feature on the GRR that gets a lot of attention, the Pentecost River crossing.

All traffic has to cross the river on a 50 yard concrete causeway, but in the water there are usually half a dozen crocodiles waiting........ just in case someone stands on the water's edge for too long, or crashes off the causeway. I would have liked to drive the whole of the GRR but we heard that the water level in the Pentecost river was high and we were also conscious that Matilda was still running well and wanted to make sure she made it back to Sydney. Reluctantly, we decided to give the main part of the GRR a miss and just tackled the first 130 km (80 miles) or so and then headed south to Windjana Gorge and then Tunnel Creek.

We were now in the limestone Napier Ranges where the Lennard River has carved a 100 yard wide gorge out of the rock leaving a channel with steep cliffs on both sides. Windjana Gorge also had a basic campsite so we set up for the night and planned to walk down the gorge in the early morning. Whilst sitting out, a warden came round. She was carrying a little bundle and showed us a baby wallaby, one whose mother had been killed alongside a nearby road. As so often happens, a mother kangaroo or wallaby is hit by a vehicle and killed, but the joey she is carrying is sometimes left alive. This one was from such an incident.

Looking in some bushes next to Matilda, we spotted a bowerbird's nest. It was only feet away from where we were parked and on the ground was a collection of stones, bottle tops and other small bits of debris. The birds were pottering about, busy attending to something important to them, but not to us, and sometimes rearranging the stones and wandering off deep into the bushes and coming back with another fragment for their nest.

In the morning, we walked off to the entrance to the gorge, and after reading warnings about crocodiles, we walked about 5 km (3 miles) down the river bank and back again. There were plenty of crocodiles about, but these were the freshwater variety better known as 'freshies' and the smaller of the two species of crocodile in Australia and which are usually harmless. They don't normally stalk or attack like their more vicious cousins, the 'saltie', but we resolved to be cautious with them no matter what – they still had powerful jaws and lots of teeth. There must have been about 50 of them during our walk and the nearest we got to them was about 10ft, although we heard someone nearby had actually been up and stroked one!

There wasn't much water in the river and we were able to walk along the sandy bank, being wary foreigners keeping an eye out for other wildlife – harmless or otherwise. I felt we should have seen other animals but all we saw were a few fruit bats hanging upside down in a bush.

Just down the road was Tunnel Creek where another river has worn away a 500m (450 yards) tunnel through the limestone rock. Here there were no guides; one just walked up from the road and wandered through, wading through knee-high water and meandering across banks of stones. There were other people about and we all had torches to see our way and to pick out the bats hanging from the ceiling. At the other end, the river discharges into open country and a path led alongside just like any tow path, but we decided to turn back and retrace our steps through the tunnel and drive on.

We soon rejoined the main road and arrived at Fitzroy Crossing, our next stop. We were now in deep Aboriginal country and in the small town there were plenty of them, but we found it very difficult to engage with them; they keep very much to themselves.

The campsite was part of a large complex that included a hotel, most of which was raised well off the ground on steel poles as a precaution against flooding in the 'Wet', the tropical rainy season. Similarly, the amenity blocks were all on raised mounds. The campsite was busy as several 4x4 tourist coaches and their charges came and went, heading into the Kimberley.

Nearby was Geikie Gorge where the Fitzroy River has cut a two mile gorge through the limestone rock. Given the campsite and hotel were raised above the floodplain, it was surprising to see how high the river can get in the Wet as the lower parts of the cliff were white, while higher up there was the normal growth of ferns, lichen and other plants.

We took a cruise down the river, a very gentle trip in an electric boat and all was peaceful, with the guide pointing out various rock formations, some of the birds and the animals. We saw several more freshies sitting on rock outcrops, and most of them slid into the water as we passed by. We also saw rock wallabies hopping about precariously on the cliffs, but seemingly surefooted enough not to become lunch for the crocodiles.

I had one last task to undertake in Fitzroy Crossing and that was a visit to the hospital for a blood test. This was easily arranged in the modern hospital, but what surprised me was that all the staff were white, whilst all the other people waiting in the Outpatients Department were Aboriginal. Enquiries revealed that almost all the patients were Aboriginal, or from the Indigenous Peoples, as they preferred to say, and they were suffering from Western diseases such as diabetes, heart conditions, obesity, and drug and alcohol related problems. It seemed to me to be a sad reflection on the European influence on noble people.

We continued along Route 1, still heading eastward, this length being called the Great Northern Highway. The tarmac road was in good condition and we were able to make rapid progress across cattle rearing country, the only interest being the occasional turn-off to a cattle station. It was nearly 320 km (200 miles) to Halls Creek where we stopped for a breather, but it was a sleepy community and we soon continued to our next stopover.

The Bungle Bungles

Back in the nineteenth century, a government surveyor was charged with inspecting the area to seek out good grazing land and noted in his journal some interesting rock formations to the north of Halls Creek. Being no good for grazing, their presence was logged in his report and filed. Thus very few people knew about the amazing rock formations until the 1980s when a film crew overflew the area and their tourist potential was realised.

The Bungle Bungles, now more properly known as Purnululu, their Aboriginal name, are protected by a national park, and although they are a long way from any major centre of civilisation, are a popular tourist destination. The park is difficult to get to, being surrounded by privately owned stations, so most people have to undertake fly-ins from nearby towns. However, one landowner has set up a caravan park and runs coach trips into the park, so we booked.

The contrasting colours of the rock domes of Purnululu National Park (formerly known as Bungle Bungles) were unknown to western eyes until the 1980s

We had found Australia to be an amazing place, but these rock formations were exceptional. The rock strata has been eroded by aeons of wind, and alternate red and black rock stripes have been left as hundreds of beehive-shaped domes. You will have seen them on travel programmes and in some films like *Australia* and they are stupendous – really amazing. Our trip was by 4x4 coach along a 60 km (40 miles) track and then around the ranges to see the first highlight of the day, Piccaninny Creek. There was no water, but when there was it has worn away the rock into long strips, a bit like giant corduroy, the dips being about nine inches deep. Fascinating.

A short walk and we entered Cathedral Gorge. The gorge has been likened to the walk into Petra in Jordan, but here a walk between the rock domes opens out into a huge chamber with a lake in the middle. Both are amongst the black and orange beehive domes that rise about 500ft above the surrounding plain. The water was very still and reflected the orange and black stripes from the surrounding rock.

Then it was a lengthy coach ride to Echidna Gorge, a deep cleft in the mountains that runs deep into the main range and at times is less than a yard wide. Finally, it was a ride back to the camp where a bush dinner was laid on for all those on the trip – we were all knackered! Truly a highlight of the trip and a terrific day.

The next day, we had a fairly short drive of 160 km (100 miles) to Kununurra, a town somewhat different to anything we had seen so far. We were now well up in the tropics and nearby Lake Argyle has been created to produce a water supply which, coupled with the Ord River Irrigation Scheme, feeds the agricultural activity in the area making it some of the most lush and productive in Australia.

The town was modern with well laid out streets, a thriving shopping centre, and very green with plenty of shady trees. There were several campsites, all full, but we eventually managed to get parked up in a dusty field at the back of one site in an overflow area. We spent a day pottering round and booked a trip to Lake Argyle.

A coach took us about 65 km (40 miles) from town to a small resort beside the lake and we decamped into a boat and, with about 40 other tourists, toured the lake with a guide providing information. The lake normally has an area of about 1,000 km^2 so in a few hours we only saw a small portion. There are 25 species of marine life, including about 25,000 freshies (we saw hundreds), and a couple of hundred species of birds nesting in the hinterland to the lake. The lake is set in low grassy hills and pootling about on the water between the hills was a pleasant way to spend a few hours.

After some lunch, we then took another boat trip down the Ord River, below the dam, into Kununurra. Again there were masses of wildlife, and it was dusk when we reached the town and were coached back to the campsite.

South of the lake is the Argyle Diamond Mine where there is an enormous deposit of a 'girl's best friend'. It is currently one of the largest producers of diamonds in the world and in town were numerous jewellery shops where, fortunately, Pam confined herself to window shopping.

Also nearby is the only known deposit of zebra stone in the world, striped rock and estimated to be 600 million years old. It was only discovered in 1924, but how it was created has baffled scientists.

We headed off towards Katherine and took a ten mile side trip to the cattle station where the mine is based. It was a rather scruffy, dusty and run-down place, probably existing on a shoestring, but a young couple were working hard to make it a success; the husband working at the opencast site, the wife, usually carrying her baby, running the small shop and adjacent campsite.

On a trip such as ours, it is easy to buy loads of mementoes to take home, but one has to be careful not to clutter up the vehicle. So far, we had managed to buy very little unless it was directly related to progressing the trip (maps and guides etc.). It was time to buy something to take home so we chose a modest piece of smooth zebra rock, a bit cheaper than a diamond!

We heard there would be a campfire at the site in the evening so later we sat out under the stars again, gently drinking the evening away and yarning with fellow campers, the flames flickering its glow on our faces. A scene that was a regular for us, but one we never tired of.

Part 7

* Katherine
* Darwin
* Murder close to home
* Mary River and Kakadu
* Understanding the Aborigines
* Daly Waters
* Mount Isa

Katherine

Katherine was our next port of call, about 512 km (320 miles) away, and we settled at a BIG4 campsite on the edge of town for a few days' R&R. It was a big site, but most pitches were under shade and we soon got talking to a couple well into their seventies who were very adventurous. They had a top specification Toyota Land Cruiser with all the bells and whistles for serious off-roading, and were towing a compact off-road camper van. Since retiring, they had undertaken a series of off-road expeditions, always heading back home to Brisbane to recover and plan the next venture. Like us, they would soon be heading out to Kakadu National Park, but unlike us they had permits to head on north through the Wellington Ranges at the western end of Arnhem Land, and on to the Cobourg Peninsula.

Also known as Garig Gunak Barlu National Park, the Cobourg Peninsula is a serious destination, and roads and tracks in the region can often be impassable for weeks on end. A permit is required to get entry to this Aboriginal territory, and another is needed to take photos or film. I wished I was joining them, but maybe another time.

Near the campsite was Katherine Warm Springs, a series of pools where the water is a steady 32C (90F) and needless to say we had a relaxing dip. It was a bit crowded but very pleasant and we spent an hour or so luxuriating in a green oasis. Later we had a look at an excellent museum on the far side of town which had yet to add a section dedicated to Katherine's most famous son, Cadel Evans, who had won the Tour de France in 2011. We scored a lot of Brownie points when we mentioned we had watched the Tour that year, spending a week of a month long trip to France in our motorhome watching the amazing cyclists tackle three stages in the Alps.

The town was a regional centre and there were numerous industrial parks on the outskirts. Matilda was suffering from the punishment we were giving her and more maintenance was needed, so first we found a locksmith who fixed the accommodation door lock, which was falling apart. No charge!

For a couple of months, a rear tyre was slowly deflating and despite several close inspections, I couldn't find the cause. So the next stop was a tyre depot where a fitter found a short tack to be causing a slow puncture. Sadly, the tyre was too damaged to repair so a new one was bought and fitted.

Of the larger towns we visited, Katherine had the highest population of Aborigines we had seen. In a bid to curb the drink problems amongst the Aborigine population, many towns ban the consumption of alcohol in public, but in Katherine we saw several of them surreptitiously knocking back cheap booze, with inevitable effects. Again, we tried to engage in conversation with a few of the sober ones, but they avoided answering and looked away so as to avoid eye contact.

While having a cup of coffee in a local bakery, we reflected on Australianisms we had encountered. Obviously the country has adopted its own version of English and many words now end in 'o', or 'ist'. So one finds:

jillaroo – female station manager

smoko – a break for a smoke or tea break

reno – house renovations

doco – documentary (on television)

bottle-o – off licence

fisho – fishmonger

vejjo – vegetarian

servo – service station

ambo – ambulance

rego – vehicle registration

removalist – house remover

funeralist – funeral director

tradey – tradesman (electrician, carpenter etc.)

also:

firies – firefighters

units – flat or apartment

burbs – suburbs

thongs – not skimpy underwear but flip flops

Manchester – linen (as it originally came from the Manchester region in the UK)

chooks – chickens

super – superannuation – all Grey Nomads talk about their super!

sticky beak – a nosey parker

Once more, it was time to move on, but before heading to Darwin, we thought we would take a look at Edith Falls on the way. It was only 50 km (30 miles) up the road and promised a lake with a major waterfall. What we hadn't reckoned on was the school holidays and the car park and campsite, where we had hoped to stay, were packed out, so we took a look at the falls from across the lake, missed a possible swim, and decided to head on. Sadly, this was after I had managed to reverse into a fellow camper's 4x4 so it cost us a bit in reparations to do this unproductive side trip!

Bush fires are an ever-present hazard and this one was beside the Stuart Highway south of Darwin

Our *Camps 6* directory listed a cheap campsite alongside a racecourse at Pussycat Flats near Pine Creek, so on name alone it was worth a visit. It proved to be a small site with motorhomes and caravans parked up amongst the stables and service buildings for the racing so we could use the showers, had power, and, just as importantly, the bar was open. As always, the locals and other campers were very friendly and it was a great place to stop.

Darwin

The run into Darwin was straightforward, gradually heading about as far north as we would get. Along the way on the Stuart Highway, we passed several old landing strips dating from World War II as the region was Australia's frontline with an invasion and bombing by the Japanese a real possibility. We found another crowded campsite on the outskirts of Darwin at Howard Springs and were allocated a rather compact pitch, but with excellent facilities, some of the best we experienced on the whole trip. It was time for another breather, so we booked a week.

It was hot and humid so we didn't feel like doing much, although we did go into Darwin a couple of times to look round, jumping from one air-conditioned building to another. I found a little garage to have Matilda's oil changed and Pam caught up on household chores and laundry. We swam a lot and attended a demonstration of didgeridoo manufacture, the Aboriginal horn-type instrument made famous by the Australian artist whose name is no longer mentioned in polite circles.

Darwin has suffered some major tragedies in the last century or so, one being bombing raids by the Japanese, and another the terrible hurricane that hit the town on Christmas Day 1974.

Australia's involvement in World War II started when nearly 200 carrier-based Japanese aircraft bombed the town in February 1942, killing 243 people. Almost 60 further raids followed over the next 18 months, during which time the fighting strength of the region was vastly improved so as to meet the foe. A considerable amount of damage was caused by the raids, and in addition to flattened buildings, shipping was sunk and allied aircraft destroyed.

Then in 1974, Cyclone Tracy hit the area, almost flattening it, and a huge airlift ensued to evacuate the majority of the town's 43,000 residents. Many died or were injured, and in the rebuilding of the town that followed, new building codes were introduced to ensure new structures would better stand up to any further cyclones.

We also visited the Australian Aviation Heritage Centre where there were numerous aircraft on display in a crowded hangar, dominated by a vast Boeing B-52 Stratocruiser bomber, originally flown by the US Air Force and donated to the museum. It was gigantic, had a wing span of 60 yards and would have used 81,000 litres of fuel just to take off. The plane was so big that the bomb bay had been converted into a small cinema.

The highlight of our stay was a late night watching a rather grainy television picture until 3.00 a.m. so as to see Andy Murray win the Wimbledon Singles Championship. We thought we were the only Poms on the site and the Australians would not be interested, but on the winning shot, a large cheer spread around the site, none louder than from Pam.

Murder close to home

As we were coming towards the end of our trip, I thought we should contact our agent, Bob Purdy, who was acting as a postal contact in Queensland for the vehicle registration authorities. We would be selling Matilda and I wanted to be sure he knew and that we followed the proper procedure. I had landline and mobile numbers for him but could get no response from either; the lines were dead. So I tried his assistant, Ferris, who had helped us through the original registration process, and after a couple of days of telephone tag, managed to speak to him.

After the usual pleasantries, I asked him, "I have been trying to get in touch with Bob but his lines seem to be disconnected."

"Haven't you heard?" came the reply.

"We've been all over the place and not kept in touch with him. We wanted to let him know that we would be back in Sydney in about four or five weeks' time and would be selling Matilda. I wanted to ask him what notification we need to give the Queensland authorities and if he needed to do anything."

"Well, I am sorry to have to tell you that Bob is dead. In fact, he was murdered on a business trip to PNG."

I was really shocked and taken aback. "My God! That's terrible."

"Yes. He was in his hotel room and there was an attempted burglary by a Papuan and it seems that in the kerfuffle a gun went off and Bob died."

Further discussion elicited that Bob had numerous business interests all over Queensland and also in PNG, Australian shorthand for Papua New Guinea, which lies about 160 km (100 miles) to the north of Cape York and is the country's closest neighbour. There are close links between the two countries, but in recent years PNG has been noted for its terrible crime rate.

Pam and I were both very shocked by this news. Although we hadn't actually met him, Bob Purdy had helped us out and now he had been murdered. Later, I went online and looked up some news stories about the incident.

Mary River and Kakadu

'Must do' places to visit around here are Kakadu and Litchfield National Parks. However, we heard that the latter was very crowded with the school holiday visitors, so we decided to head for Kakadu, a huge area to the east of this part of the Northern Territory. It wasn't too far to the delightfully named Humpty Doo on the Arnhem Highway, and we headed on to Corroboree Tavern for a coffee and booked an afternoon trip on the nearby Mary River, as well as a night in the caravan park to the back of the tavern.

At the time of year we visited, Mary River wasn't a river at all, but a series of billabongs and wetlands, and the main attraction was the birdlife, although there were several salties about as well. The boat held about 30 people and the sides were built up with mesh just in case a crocodile should think about having a closer look at the occupants than was healthy! The largest we saw was about 15 foot long, and as we approached he was sitting on a bank, but effortlessly slipped into the water, and within moments all we could see were a couple of nodules from his knobbly back.

A saltwater crocodile takes a keen interest in our boat on the Mary River, NT

What's more, he was facing the boat – just in case a feeding opportunity arose! Amongst the reeds and leaf debris in the water, one wouldn't know he was there, but with 78 teeth and a jaw with massive strength, they are not creatures to tamper with!

The guide took the boat just about as far as possible up the various creeks and inlets, and we were able to see umpteen samples of the local birdlife including:

- *white-breasted sea eagles*

- *jabiru*

- *brolga*

- *kingfishers*

- *intermediate egrets*

- *data bird*

- *pied cormorant*

- *pied heron*

- *magpie geese*

- *corn-crested jacana*

- *radjah shelducks*

- *whistling kites*

- *azure kingfisher*

- *forest kingfisher*

- *pelican*

- *grey brolga*

- *great egrets*

- *black-faced cuckooshrike*

- *Jesus bird so named because it appears to be able to walk on water, but is actually on water lilies. The real name is comb-crested jacana*

and probably a few more we didn't get to list in our little notebook. It was a terrific selection of birdlife and most of the specimens we saw were close up and easily photographed. Bill Oddie would be in his element!

We also saw agile wallaby, but with so much water around, they were some distance away.

Out in the marshes, buffalo can be a major problem and can be almost as vicious as a crocodile. They were introduced to the region in the nineteenth century as a farm animal from Indonesia but inevitably some escaped into the wilderness and a substantial wild population became established. They cause a significant amount of environmental damage, and capturing them for their meat and hides remains a worthy but dangerous occupation.

We saw none in the wild but on returning to the tavern, they had a couple in a rather basic enclosure, with a saltie in a small enclosure next door. We hoped they stayed there while we stopped the night.

We got chatting to a local about the potential the region has for the future development of Australia. We had heard the Government wanted to harness the water from the four main rivers in the area to create a new agricultural sector that would have the expanding south-east Asian market on its doorstep.

Apparently there had been a similar scheme in the 1950/'60s which had started with great hopes but foundered when nature bit back and nobody could make any money out of their investments. The area between Darwin and Arnhem Land lies in the floodplain of one or other of the rivers and potentially should be able to produce fertile land for agricultural development.

In the early 1950s, a group of investors, mainly from California but also including Australia's first proper investment bank, surveyed the area with the idea of growing rice to feed the Asian market and set up the Territory Rice Limited which would be based at Humpty Doo. The Australian government official involved was Harold Holt who later went on to become Australia's Premier, and who strangely vanished while swimming on a remote beach in South Australia after just two years in post.

Other than the Aborigines, virtually nobody used the land and there were few roads, power lines or other facilities. Because at the time the Aborigines were non-persons, they weren't consulted, although they lived off the land and had done for generations.

The government invested in infrastructure and built an airstrip and a dam to catch rainwater during the Wet. However, the project lacked sufficient finance from the outset and rice growing proved to be more difficult than had been thought. The project lasted only a few years and finally closed in the early 1960s. The region did however benefit from the infrastructure that had been put in place which in time brought in tourists and allowed some limited development along the road leading towards Arnhem Land.

The dams that were built, the Fogg and the nearby Harrison Dams, have both become wildlife reserves and one can take tours and spot all manner of local flora and fauna. Fogg Dam has its own resident crocodile inevitably called Phileas Fogg, Jules Verne's main character in his book, *Around the World in Eighty Days*.

The local we were talking to was very dismissive of the plans to develop the region. Whilst more modern approaches to such a scheme might improve the possibilities of success, there are great environmental concerns and worries about the impact any scheme might have on the indigenous people. He also felt it would be hard to attract workers to the area because it is so hot and humid, making for a very difficult working environment.

Interestingly along here is the Alligator River, but there are no alligators in Australia, are there? Early explorers apparently named the river after the creatures they found there, not knowing they were crocodiles.

In the morning, we pulled into the Bark Hut Inn for fuel and I was presented with a pleasant surprise. In drove half a dozen old Chevrolet cars, five from the 1920s, the other a later model from the 1930s. These were no ordinary classic cars, they were all highly modified for remote travel and the drivers told me they took delight in touring the 'outer' Outback, heading down what most people would describe as cart tracks, a practice known as bush bashing here. The cars had uprated suspensions, modified engines and towed camping trailers, one even had a winch mounted at the front. They took trips to sample the old days of Australian motoring and to relive the early days when the country was being opened up. They looked well-travelled and I suspect they were returning from the remoter parts of Arnhem Land, maybe even the Cobourg Peninsula. This is how old cars should be used, not cosseted in cotton wool and kept in museums. Good luck to them and their travels.

Nearby we visited the Mamakala Wetlands, just a few miles off the highway and spent some time at an observation platform overlooking a large wetland area hoping to see some interesting wildlife. It must have been a quiet day as we saw almost no birds at all. However, we did take a 4 km (3 mile) walk around nearby countryside amongst paperbark and pandanus trees that lined the edge of the wetland. Again, we saw little of interest but felt better for the exercise.

Jabiru, our destination for the day, was a soulless mining town established to service the needs of nearby uranium mining leases. The location illustrates the dilemma that is faced by the authorities in Australia as there are huge mineral deposits but they seem to be in areas of great environmental importance. Do you mine, or do you protect the environment and the fauna and flora?

The next day, we turned south and effectively started our long journey back to Sydney.

The journey back through the national park took us through lush tropical forests and with quiet roads we could often see wildlife in the bush – wild donkey, dingoes, emu and, of course, kangaroos.

We stopped at Nourlangie to take a look at some Aborigine rock art and learn something of their culture from the park guide who showed us round. We met our guide on a rocky outcrop and she explained that the range of hills across the wide valley were sacred to the indigenous population but the mining companies wanted to exploit their reserves as well. We weren't far from the mines near Jabiru and here, potentially, was the next plot to be turned into a huge opencast mine.

A walking tour followed and we passed through several galleries of rock art, walking on broad walks between each. Coach parties had begun to arrive, the numbers of people had increased, and their presence took away the quiet seclusion of the place.

At Anbangbang, there was a rock overhang providing shelter to the indigenous residents and it was estimated they had been coming here for 20,000 years. There was much rock art here, now protected from human reach and touch, one interesting painting being of a thylacine, better known as the Tasmanian tiger. This variety of wolf with a striped back became extinct on mainland Australia about 2,500 years ago, and on Tasmania as recently as the 1930s, when the last known example died in a zoo.

Understanding the Aborigines

I have mentioned earlier about the history of the Aborigines, or Indigenous Peoples, as they are sometimes referred to. It was only after visiting Kakadu that the overall picture of their background began to come clear, and I was beginning to understand their psyche.

We had learned about their presence in Australia in various Visitor Information Centres, art exhibitions, and museums and heard from guides, park wardens and others, and it was much the same story each time. The Aborigines had been in Australia for a long time, it was their land and their environmental impact was non-existent. Then the Europeans had arrived and they had been turfed off the land, in many cases they had been incarcerated, their children taken away, and much more.

But it was the Dreamtime, the way of thinking of Aborigines, that was now becoming clearer, although still somewhat of a mystical concept. It is estimated the original humans arrived on the Australian continent from the north as long as 60,000 years ago. At the time, it is thought that Indonesia was connected by land to Australia and the first peoples to venture south eventually inhabited the whole continent as well as Tasmania.

When the first Europeans arrived in the eighteenth century, there were nearly 400 tribes or clans and innumerable languages.

However, they all lived more or less in harmony, living off the land and the indigenous flora and fauna. They had learned to use fire to their advantage and would sometimes burn off the land to stimulate further growth of plants.

There has never been any evidence of any permanent buildings being constructed by the Aborigines and the only lasting features they left on the land were modest rock paintings, some of which still exist and we had seen.

Their approach to life was ethereal and based on stories and histories passed down from generation to generation by clan and family elders. And 60,000 years represents something like 2,500 generations of Aborigines, so the stories represent what we would think of as an oral library of history, geography, family events, heroes and villains, and much more. By geography, I am meaning the lay of the land, where the best waterholes were, the boundaries of clan territory, where to find animals, interpreting the weather, all of which were vital to life in a sometimes hostile environment.

Native people didn't go to a library or have reference books for help and advice, and couldn't have imagined something like the Internet or Google, but held all this information in their minds and it is this somewhat nebulous mental picture of their country, life, history, traditions, spiritual beliefs and myths, especially those myths relating to animals, that is the Dreaming or Dreamtime. I am sure the Aborigines could teach us a lot.

Daly Waters

We headed back to Route 1 and the Stuart Highway, or The Track as Northern Territorians call it, passing Pussycat Flats where we had camped previously, and spent the night in Katherine again. Then it was on south to Daly Waters.

So many people had said we must go to Daly Water, we really couldn't give it a miss, and we were glad we didn't. Daly Waters is a small community, originally based around an aerodrome now only used in emergencies, and where there is an old Outback pub. The community is only a few miles off the Stuart Highway so is easy to get to and thus it attracts a lot of visitors.

Our drive down from Katherine was routine, except for an incident where a very thin, elderly gentleman wearing the briefest of briefs jumped out in front of us as we bowled along. Why he did so, and who he was, we never found out, but he looked raving mad. We had no intention of stopping and carried on.

It's about 280 km (175 miles) from Katherine to Daly Waters so it is a sensible day's run and we were able to stop at Mataranka for a coffee in a small art gallery. It was a pleasant stop as the art gallery was quiet and the tables set out for refreshments were attracting colourful blue-faced honeyeaters. The birds are also known as banana birds and are black, white and a golden olive-green. In addition, the ones we saw had a blue flash of colour over their eyebrows making them a very attractive bird to watch at close quarters.

Arriving at Daly Waters, though, we were astonished at how busy it was and we were lucky to get into the campsite next to the pub, although only at a non-powered pitch next to the toilets.

We took a walk round and the pub was much the same as others in the Outback with lots of odd memorabilia, including at least 100 bras adorning the walls and ceiling and some jokey signs. Nearby was a dilapidated shop selling knick-knacks, mostly irreverent, on the roof of which was the rusted hulk of an old helicopter. It was that sort of place.

We chatted with the owner of the shop, and he must have noted my Isle of Man T-shirt as later he came on stage as one of the acts for the evening show in the pub and he made reference to my presence. It was a great show with three performers and a lot of self-deprecating Australian humour coupled with a good meal. We could see why the place is so popular.

In the morning, the caravan site had emptied almost completely by the time we were ready to go at 9.15 a.m., but I am sure there was another shift of tourists heading there for the next show later in the day.

On our way back to the Stuart Highway, we stopped off to take a look at the Stuart Tree. When John Stuart, after whom the highway was named, was exploring this region, he supposedly carved his initial into a tree to mark the spot on his third attempt to reach the far north coast at what is now Darwin. A rather blackened stump of a tree remains and the letter 'S' can just be made out.

Almost alongside is Daly Waters Airfield with a hangar and outbuildings and a sealed runway now riddled with weeds and small bushes. The runway was originally built as a staging and refuelling stop for the 1926 London – Sydney Air Race and then for early QANTAS flights to Singapore. With the outbreak of World War II, it was taken over by the air force.

For us it was time to head off into remote areas again and rather than head south on the main highway to Three Ways and then east to Mount Isa, we went due east on the Carpentaria Highway with the plan of going 269 km (170 miles) to Cape Crawford and then 373 km (233 miles) south to Barkly Homestead. We stopped at Cape Crawford for fuel and, once we had put on our blue suede shoes, took a look at the Heartbreak Hotel, the only notable building in the area. Elvis was out! One might expect that Cape Crawford was near the sea, but it would be another 150 km (95 miles) to get to the Gulf of Carpentaria, had we so wanted.

We went south on the long run across the Barkly Tablelands in fine weather but with lots of cattle-carrying road trains. The Tablelands Highway was almost all single track with wide gravel verges on each side. When we could see another car coming the other way, it was a game of chicken to see who would veer to the side so as to run one set of wheels on the gravel, keeping the offside set on the tarmac. With combined speeds of 100 to 120 mph, it wasn't a game to take casually, but was fun all the same and seemed to work.

The real problem was with road trains. They give way to nobody and would stay on the tarmac come what may; we then had to get right over onto the gravel and hope to keep going in a straight line and not get caught up in a slide. Throw in a few road ditches and marker posts, and the heart was pounding.

About halfway to the Barkly Homestead, there was a lay-by identified in the *Camps 6* directory that looked a good stopover for the night, but when we got there we found the artesian well head adjacent to the parking area creaked and groaned, so we headed on. A little further on, near Walhallow Station, the map showed some unmade tracks leading off east so we headed down them hoping to find a camp spot. Very soon we ended up in a maze of tracks but nowhere suitable for a stop so headed back to the main highway and on south to another junction, this time at the start of a stock route leading to Anthony Lagoon Station.

We pulled off the track and parked clear of the road to set up for the night. I had a plan to sit out later and admire the southern skies and the wondrous Milky Way. We were miles from anywhere and we expected a quiet, undisturbed night, but it wasn't to be. Road train after road train arrived on the main highway and turned down the stock route towards the station only to return a few hours later loaded with cattle, presumably heading for the meatworks.

More cattle trucks woke us early in the morning so we made a prompt start and continued on south. Within 20 miles, we came to a junction where a road sign summed up the remoteness of where we were and the hardships that must be endured by those making a living here. A well graded track to the east led to Calvert Hills Station – it was 264 km (165 miles) away! From where we stood, it was about 160 km (100 miles) to a main road, and nearly 480 km (300 miles) to Mount Isa, the next town of any size. That's almost 900 km (565 miles) - and there are no shortcuts!

We had an uneventful trip down to the main road at the Barkly Homestead, had a breather and headed on towards Mount Isa. The road we were on now was much busier as it is the main route across the north of Australia, and by late afternoon we had crossed the border into Queensland, put our clocks half an hour forward, and stopped for the night in Camooweal. We only just got a pitch on a site as the first was full, and several people were heading for the second, but we just got in first.

Mount Isa

There was nothing to keep us in Camooweal so in the morning we headed straight on to Mount Isa, the major regional town and a centre for mining activities. The mining works for copper, zinc, silver and lead became very apparent as we neared the town and we could see tall chimneys discharging steam over the surrounding landscape.

We took the opportunity of being in 'civilisation' to top up our food stocks and to Skype our daughters, the one in Sydney, and also our younger daughter, Sue, in Folkestone back home. We learned some great news; Sue was pregnant again with number two! Later we drank a toast to her and husband, Bradley, as well as number one, Isobelle, and of course, the unnamed number two.

A jabiru taking flight as we drive past in Matilda

We stayed one night, joining other campers in a cook up of meat balls and rolls organised by the site owners, and the next day continued along the Barkly Highway to Cloncurry for a break. In the coffee shop, we got talking to a couple who had lived in Narrabeen (in Sydney where we had spent a month) almost next door to the campsite and although we never got round to talking about it, one wonders why they should now be living in such a remote part of Queensland.

Refreshed, we noticed a huge pall of smoke to the east of town and learned that a road train had caught fire, blocking the road. It was fortunate we were heading the other way, and we soon found the road out of town to the north on the Matilda Highway and started out towards Normanton.

A road train seen near Normanton, QLD

Roughly halfway up to Normanton is the Burke and Wills Roadhouse so we stopped for lunch before heading on. The roadhouse is named after Robert Burke and William Wills who are Australian heroes and did much to open up the hinterland of Australia in the mid-nineteenth century. In 1860, they led an expedition with the aim of crossing the centre of Australia on a north/south route starting in Melbourne and heading for the Gulf of Carpentaria, which was about 192 km (120 miles) up the road from where we were parked.

The expedition was very well equipped, taking more than 20 horses, numerous wagons loaded with food for two years, and 26 camels. With 19 men, they had to cross nearly 3,200 km (2,000 miles) of unexplored territory through the centre of the continent and inevitably they suffered all sorts of privations. Progress was slow, and with such a large party, it was agreed to leave a group behind at

Coopers Creek, near what is now Innamincka, with a smaller party heading for the north. Those remaining behind were instructed to stay for 13 weeks and then return south.

Further privations ensued and eventually the mangrove swamps prevented Burke and Wills from reaching the actual water's edge of the Gulf and they had to stop a few miles short of their target.

The return journey south was very difficult and the men had to shoot some of their animals to feed themselves. Having reached Coopers Creek camp, they found that their colleagues had already left, but had buried some supplies below a tree which they'd had the foresight to mark. Sadly, the party had left only hours before the Burke and Wills group arrived. They received some help with food from local Aborigines, but it was their undoing as they failed to cook it properly. The food led to their dying in the bush of thiamine poisoning and only one member of the original party that made it to the Gulf survived.

It is a tragic tale and but for a slight change in circumstances would have been praised for its magnificent achievement. The bodies of Burke and Wills were eventually recovered and they were given a proper funeral in Melbourne attended by tens of thousands of people. The tree, near Coopers Creek, became known as the Dig Tree and, despite catching fire a couple of times, is now a national monument.

It was time for us to head on for the Gulf and we drove further up the Matilda Highway to a *Camps 6* recommended spot where joined a South Australian couple for an evening's yarning before settling down for the night. They had sold up their farm, put their possessions into store, and were travelling round until they got fed up or found somewhere to settle down and enjoy the rest of their retirement.

In the morning, we soon got to Normanton, a sleepy town beside the Norman River. This is crocodile country and in the main street there was a fibreglass replica of what is claimed to be the largest ever estuarine crocodile. It was shot in 1957, weighed about two tons and was 8.63m (28ft) long. Not a beast to meet on a dark night!

Part 8

* Karumba
* Flat Creek Station
* Cooktown
* Meeting the Quayles
* Parting of the ways
* Home run

Karumba

It was only a short run to Karumba, a small town at the mouth of the Norman River. It is a popular spot for Grey Nomads as it is about as far north as one can go on tarmac roads, and it lies on the Gulf of Carpentaria so offers great fishing opportunities plus the town faces west so there are great sunsets.

We booked into a site and as the town is fairly spread out, we took a drive round ending up at The Point where we watched the sunset and had a drink at the nearby Sunset Tavern. Outside the pub, several people were involved in setting up gazebos and putting up bunting and flags and other bits and pieces, and we found out there was to be a charity event at the pub the next day linked to the Melbourne Cup. There would be a couple of hundred people there so we thought it would be worthwhile staying on an extra day to join the fun.

We made a leisurely start in the morning as we were beginning to get a bit travel weary. Our travels over the last few months were finally catching up with us and whilst we were still having a whale of a time and enjoying the country, the scenery and people, a few days' break would have been welcome.

We finally made it out to The Point and there were already 200 people gathered at the pub for the Karumba Cancer Cuppa Event based around the Melbourne Cup, which was visiting the town for the day and was the focus of activities.

To say the Melbourne Cup is Australia's major horse race is really an injustice as it is much more than that. The race takes place at the Flemington Racecourse in Melbourne during the first week of November each year and brings the whole country to a stop. It is the Derby, Grand National and Prix de l'Arc de Triomphe all rolled into one. The big day is a Bank Holiday in some states and many people take the day off to hold a BBQ, drink some beer, well usually quite a lot of beer, and place a few bets.

Back in Karumba, many of the locals were dressed up for the occasion with the women wearing their poshest frocks, usually topped off with a fascinator, the men in their smart clothes and best shoes. By late morning, when we turned up, the event was in full flow, the drink was plentiful and gradually cash was being wheedled out of the pockets of punters in the aid of the charity. There were raffles, prizes for the best dressed, a hobby horse race, and more.

Not dressed in our finest, we took a place on the periphery of things and joined a group of Australians who had also decided to dress down and were also travelling the country like us. Apart from a short break when we were over the road for a huge fish and chip lunch at the highly recommended Ashes restaurant, we were there all day.

At the bar I was keen to find out more about what was going on and happened to ask a smartly dressed woman who seemed to be part of the organising group. She turned out to be Sheila Laxon, originally from Pontypridd in Wales, who had been the first woman trainer to win the Melbourne Cup when her horse *Ethereal* won the event in 2001. She was now based in Victoria and gave us a hot tip for the race in 2014.

Sheila also explained the nature of the event we were at. To help raise funds for cancer charities, the actual Melbourne Cup, a huge gold goblet, was taken around the country to remote communities and used, like today, as the basis for fundraising activities. Sheila was there for the day, as was a senior member of the Royal Victoria Racing Club who organise the race. We had our photo taken with Sheila and the Cup for the princely sum of A$5.

As the day wore on, so the level of donations increased in line with the amount of beer being consumed. We attend lots of charity fundraising events through our involvement with Lions Clubs International, and I noted a great idea for organising raffles. So often one buys a strip of raffle tickets and when the draw takes place, the first person to win takes the prize they want, as does the second place. And so on, until those at the end are left with a choice of prizes nobody else wants – cheap toiletries, unusual, evil-looking chocolates or biscuits, weird undrinkable spirits bought during a drunken moment on holiday, unwanted gifts, and so on.

Here there were a huge number of raffle prizes ranging from an iPad down to some of the same ilk as above. But in front of each prize was a sealed bucket with a slot in the top. One bought tickets for the draw and put your ticket in the bucket(s) for prizes you actually wanted to win. Thus the iPad attracted two buckets full of tickets, and the buckets for bottles of odd-looking spirits accumulated hardly enough tickets to cover the bottom.

By early evening, the event was drawing to a close. We had won nothing in the raffle, and like everyone else we were quite merry and, not wanting to drive in the dark (our sidelights weren't working), we decided to head back to the campsite in daylight, but needn't have worried about the local police as we later learned that most were at the event, or had the day off. A bit of drink driving wasn't taken too seriously on a day like this in a remote corner of Australia!

It was time to move on and leave the sea for a few days and head east across the base of Cape York. The trip up to Cape York, the northernmost point in Australia, is another of the great 4x4 trips and it was one I would have liked to have tackled. However, with our unexpected delay in Sydney earlier in the year, we no longer had the time. Maybe on another visit to Australia.

Our route retraced our trip from Normanton, where we stopped for fuel, before heading out along the Gulflander Development Road towards Georgetown. The road follows the railway for much of the way, although we never saw a train. We saw our first wild cat along here, feeding off some roadkill until we came close when it headed off into the bush. Not long after, we came across a long-necked turtle, only about six inches long, walking along the verge. We stopped and could see that its shell had some damage, perhaps from being hit by a car. There was no sign of any water, where these creatures should be found, so we had no choice but to leave him there to his destiny.

The Gulflander Railway stops at Croydon, so we did too, and had lunch beside a reservoir at the back of town where we could see numerous water fowl going about their daily business. Croydon was yet another town that had its heyday when the gold mines thrived, but now is just a transit town on the road, and a local commercial centre.

Travelling along towards Georgetown, we came up behind a road train trundling along, only we noticed quite quickly that it was meandering back and forth across the road. The road, like so many in Australia, was straight as a die but led us over low crests that were blind to oncoming traffic. It was clear the driver was either falling asleep, or perhaps distracted by his mobile phone or something else.

The thought of him hitting an oncoming vehicle and the carnage that would result was more than we wanted to contemplate but there was little we could do. He veered back and forth across the highway occasionally catching the verge on the nearside, noticeable by the spray of dust and dirt that flew into the air. In fact, doing this seemed to bring the driver round as for a while he was running straight, but what would happen if we started to overtake? We kept our distance for a while but soon he started veering around again. I sounded Matilda's horn, but quite frankly it was a pretty weak squeak, and I also flashed the headlights.

In the end, we had no choice so we started to overtake, all the while as we drew alongside sounding the horn and flashing the headlights, and fortunately the vehicle stayed pretty straight. As I pulled alongside the cab, I hoped we might be able to look up to the driver and give him some signal of our concern, but Pam, on the nearside and nearest, couldn't see him.

I pulled well ahead before moving back to the nearside and fortunately there was no traffic for a long way ahead. We headed on and crossed our fingers in the hope that the road train driver would stop and have a sleep.

We drove on to Georgetown coming across numerous kangaroo on the road, and then stopped for the night at a rather grim caravan park. In the morning, we went to the Ted Elliott Mineral Collection, an amazing display of some 4,500 mineral specimens collected together from all over the world. It was far more interesting than we expected.

Flat Creek Station

It had always been part of our plan to find a cattle station to stay at for a day or two, but somehow it had never happened. In Georgetown, by chance I picked up a leaflet for a local cattle station at Flat Creek, so we thought we would give it a go.

The station was approached along a 50 km (30 miles) gravel road with regular drops into dried up creeks and a couple of gates to open and close. The campground had limited facilities with no power, a basic amenity block, and hot water provided from a donkey boiler, and we just drove in and chose our own spot to park up. By British standards, the cattle station was huge, 30,000 acres, and we found that most people staying there were fossicking for gold. An old gold mining town, MacDonald, of which almost nothing remains, was nearby and there was still scope to make a find if you had a decent metal detector, and a bit of luck.

Flat Creek was a nice and relaxing place, and we took some bush walks, and nearly trod on a walleroo that was resting under a low bush. Walleroos are a type of kangaroo and this guy was about 7 ft tall and had huge chunky hips. We also took a tour round the station with Peter, one of the owners. This included a visit to the homestead where they are breeding Gouldian finches, a very colourful bird that can be found locally, but is at risk of becoming extinct. We did some bird watching at a billabong and ended up at a local view spot to watch the sunset, inevitably while supping some wine.

A couple of red kangaroos seen in the evening light on
Flat Creek Station, QLD

Fossicking can be a profitable hobby; one fossicker had found a lump of gold about the size of his little finger that was worth about A$2,000, but it had taken him three visits to find it. As you may imagine, we called him Goldfinger. Another had several smaller finds but they were still worth several thousand dollars.

We stayed two nights and as the road out would probably be our last lengthy stretch of gravel road, and as it was smooth and fairly twisty, I thought I would have a final thrash in Matilda. Not too fast, but enough to make the driving interesting with some drifting through the corners. It was great and for nearly 50 km (30 miles) I thoroughly enjoyed myself – even Pam had a smile on her face when we arrived at the tarmac.

An endangered Gouldian finch at Flat Creek Station, QLD, where they are being bred for release into the wild

We had been in savannah country, mainly scrub with low trees and huge termite mounds, but as we headed east we were entering tropical countryside with very green, lush growth. Australians are very protective of their flora and fauna, as anyone who has seen the television programme *Border Control* will find. In this part of the country, they take things a stage further and there are free vehicle washes to clean vehicles, particularly their underside, so as to wash off potentially harmful weeds and seeds that they do not want spread around the region. We came upon one of these washes near Mount Surprise, and, like most people, drove through it a couple of times.

Within only a few miles, the countryside was becoming more like home with dense foliage and tall trees. We headed north to Atherton and stayed a couple of nights, taking a long walk over hills at the back of the site and also taking time to catch up on our shopping. On the road we had passed a cyclist and beeped him as we drove by, receiving a friendly wave in return. While Pam was shopping, I saw him outside the supermarket and found out he was English and had been cycling around Australia, getting lifts occasionally and just taking his time to enjoy the scenery, at a slower pace than us.

We headed on to Mareeba, passing banana and coffee plantations and stopped to visit a coffee museum and tasting establishment. The museum at Coffee Works had hundreds of items of paraphernalia linked to coffee, coffee roasting machines, coffee pots, and much more, and there were opportunities to sample about 20 varieties of coffee, liqueurs and also chocolate drinks. It was all quite interesting but I must have tried too many samples as later in the day I felt all 'coffeed out' and I couldn't face any more coffee for several weeks, in fact until we got back to the UK.

Cooktown

The roads had been pretty busy around Atherton and Mareeba, but once we passed the turning to Cairns and carried on north, it thinned out, and at Mt Molloy where we turned onto the Cooktown road, there was even less traffic. It was here that we had a choice of route. I considered whether to head down to the coast and take a 4x4 route to Cooktown via Cape Tribulation. It was off Cape Trib, as it is known locally, that Captain Cook fell foul of the Great Barrier Reef and nearly lost his ship. I had carried out some research on the road, which would also have given us a chance to visit the Daintree Forest National Park, but the route was very steep and narrow with very tight turns, and a couple of people reckoned that Matilda would struggle.

So we took the main road, which was very scenic with a couple of small pockets of habitation. One was at Lakeland where there was a roadhouse and also the turning to Laura, effectively the starting point for most people heading up to Cape York.

Bowling along the road to Cooktown, we were following some cars and suddenly they were weaving back and forth across the road in front of us. They were swerving to avoid a snake on the road, and we were forced to do the same to avoid running over it. I stopped as quickly as I could to walk back to take a photograph but, although the verge was a good ten metres wide on both sides, there was no sign of it. From the colour and length, I suspect it was another western brown.

The caravan site was on the edge of town and we were soon socialising with our neighbouring travellers. These included a clutch (is that the right word?) of classic tractor enthusiasts who were due to start a trip to Cape York and back, a distance of 1,500 km (950 miles) all on gravel roads, which would take them several weeks as they were so slow. There were about 20 of them and they came from all over Australia and did similar challenging trips every couple of years.

We took a visit to the James Cook Museum and it provided an insightful record of Cook's time in the area. When his ship grounded on Endeavour Reef, he had to jettison much of the heavier items of cargo so as to refloat his ship. The museum displays the original anchor and a cannon which were only retrieved from the depths a few years ago. They also have the stump of the tree to which *HMS Endeavour* was supposedly tied during the seven-week stay in the area to undertake the repair work. There was a great deal of information about the scientific work undertaken by Josef Banks, the ship's botanist. It was here in Cooktown that the crew first saw kangaroos and what they called alligator because they had no knowledge of crocodiles. I thought it odd that no mention had been made in the displays of the crew's thoughts on the snakes of Australia, but apparently they never saw any of them.

Eventually, Cook had done all he could to repair his ship and it was time to head on with his voyage. Leaving the river mouth proved very tricky and Cook didn't want to fall prey to the coral reefs again and was glad to make open water. Sailing on north, he very nearly came to grief again, but eventually sailed beyond the northern tip of Australia to land on a small island that became known as Possession Island. Realising he had now travelled up the eastern coast of what became Australia, Cook recognised it was time to claim the newly-found land for the British Crown and on Wednesday 22nd August 1770, he wrote in his log:

Notwithstanding I had in the Name of His Majesty taken possession of several places upon this coast, I now once more hoisted English Coulers (colours) and in the Name of His Majesty King George the Third took possession of the whole Eastern Coast ….. together with all the Bays, Harbours, Rivers and Islands situate upon the said coast.

Three shots were fired in the air to mark the occasion and these were answered by three further shots from *Endeavour*.

Cook had not been entirely fair in his dealings with the local population. In his instructions from King George III, he had been requested to investigate the land then known as New Holland and *"with the permission of the peoples"* to claim it for Britain. This he clearly failed to do but all the same Cook would be remembered as having 'discovered' Australia, and both the Dutch and French had missed their chance.

Here in Cooktown, Cook had extensive contact with the local indigenous population, and noted their simple lifestyle and lack of personal possessions. He also saw how very concerned they became when they saw he kept caged birds on board. They thought they should be freed, and they showed no interest in various gifts of beads and similar items that were left out for them.

This caused Cook to write in his journal:

They (indigenous peoples) may appear to soewm (some) to be the most wretched people on Earth, but in reality they are far more happier than we Europeans: being wholy unacquainted not only with the superfluos but the necessary Conveniences so much sought after in Europe, they are happy in not knowing the use of them. They live in

Tranquility which is not disturb'd by the Inequality of Condition. The Earth and sea of their own accord furnishes them with all the things necessary for life .... They seem't to set no value upon any thing we gave them, nor would they ever part with any thing of their own for any one article we would offer them; this in my opinion argues they think themselves provided with all the necessarys of life.

How sad it is that these people were to suffer so badly at the hands of Europeans for two centuries, and only recently has it been recognised that they were the original inhabitants and their land (the whole of Australia) was stolen from them.

We stayed a few days in Cooktown and it had a lovely lazy, laid-back feel to it. The view across the river to the mangrove swamps and on to distant hills was dreamy.

The Cooktown Hotel is a typical Australian pub

We drank with locals in one of the pubs and admired the fine buildings along the main street which had been built during the years of the gold boom.

Beginning the journey south to Cairns and beyond had the feel of the beginning of the end of our adventure in Australia. We headed back south on the road we had used to get to Cooktown, taking a diversion to the Lions Den Hotel, another Outback pub that was full of character. We had a drink and watched a couple of olive-backed sunbirds building a nest on the edge of the roof just above our heads. We stopped at Lakeland again for fuel and decided to stop the night further on at Mt Molloy where the locals have set up a camping area at the edge of the village where there were about 40 rigs parked up. It was clearly a well-used site – at home, it would be called a traveller's site!

An olive-backed sunbird nest building at the Lions Den Hotel near Cooktown, QLD

In the morning, we left for Port Douglas on the coast. The town is a busy upmarket tourist destination and it was bustling with a Sunday market in full flow. We took a look round and then headed on south along the coast road to Cairns, mostly alongside various beaches and headlands. The road was very busy, such a change from our experiences over recent months, but we were soon in Cairns and booked into the BIG4 campsite.

Meeting the Quayles

My surname, Quayle, is fairly unusual and originates from the Isle of Man where I was born, where it is a relatively common name. In Cairns, we came across the name for the first time in Australia when checking into the campsite, and it proved to be something of a weird experience.

"Can we book in for a week please?" I asked.

"No problem. What name is it?"

"Quayle. Vic Quayle."

"Oh, are you here for the Quayle family convention?"

"The what?"

"We've already had two Quayles check in today. Are you with them?"

"No, we aren't, but we'll have to make sure we get in touch with them. What pitch are they on?"

"I'm sorry, I can't give you that information – you know, data protection and all that stuff."

I didn't press the point but somehow we would have to work out a way of making contact with potential very distant relatives.

The site was unusual in that rather than mark our pitch on a site plan and point us in the right direction, the receptionist took us on a tour of the site in a golf buggy. It was time to find out more about the Quayles so as we were touring round, I asked, "So if you can't tell me which pitch the Quayles are on, how about some yes or no answers?"

"Try me."

"Let's do it the hard way. Are they on pitch number one?"

"Yes."

"You're joking?"

"No. They really are, and we have over two hundred pitches, so it's just as well you started at the beginning." I couldn't believe it had been so easy, although it could just as easily have been a long Q&A session.

We set ourselves up and I went over to pitch one where I introduced myself and got talking to a family of four, two adults and two children. They couldn't believe they were actually speaking to someone from the Isle of Man because they knew their family had originally come from there, but their knowledge of the island was limited. The family were from Melbourne and visiting with his widowed mother who was the other Quayle and had checked in and was staying in a cabin. We arranged to meet up for a chat the next evening and had a good time swapping notes about the Quayles of Australia and those back at home.

Parting of the ways

Cairns would see the parting of the ways for Pam and me; it really was the end of our adventure. The plan was to spend time preparing Matilda for sale, do some more tourist activity and Pam was to fly south to Sydney for some grandmother practice while I drove down so we both spent time with our family before flying home to the UK.

We cleaned up Matilda inside and out and gave her bodywork a polish. There were a number of blemishes on the fibreglass bodywork, most from stones being thrown up from the road, and we had these repaired. By chance, we also met up with an auto electrician who was working on a caravan nearby and he came over to try and get our sidelights working. He poked and jiggled the wiring about but couldn't find any obvious cause; however, when I tried the lights out later, they worked. Bingo.

I also asked the electrician if he knew someone who could fix the broken drawer we had inside the van and he put us in touch with a kitchen specialist in town. The electrician had obviously popped in there before I arrived as when I walked in with the drawer, the boss said, "No problem, we can have a look at that." An assistant undid all the screws and pulled the drawer apart, got new fittings and put it together and it was as good as new. What's more, they wouldn't take anything for it, as, apparently the boss was a motorbike fan and I came from the Isle of Man. Nuf said. I put a A$20 note in the beer fund.

The campsite put on two events while we were there – a cheese and biscuit get-together where we met more locals, and a poetry evening with a couple of poets, one of whom was very funny and irreverent. Pam also found out about a Masters sports tournament being held at various venues around Cairns and we went and watched some netball and tennis.

Cairns is the starting point for what is now a tourist railway that climbs up a steep escarpment through tunnels and cuttings as well as over bridges and viaducts ending at the hill resort of Kuranda. It was an interesting trip and we spent the day there before returning via a cable car system back down to town. Kuranda was very busy with tourists, the majority of whom seemed to be Japanese, but we soon found a signed walk through the local tropical forest which we took, and managed to escape the madding crowd. We also had a chance encounter with a honeyeater perched on top of a short tree stump doing a mating dance, although we couldn't see the target of his affections.

Home run

On our last night, our adventure before dementia more or less over, we went into town for a celebratory meal. The next day, Pam caught a plane down to Sydney to stay with our daughter and her family. I stayed one more night and then headed off to journey south. It would be 2,800 km (1,750 miles) and I planned to take my time and spend about a week on the trip.

Except for the last night and final run into Sydney, it was an uneventful journey down. After a drive along the picturesque coast road from Cairns through mile upon mile of cane plantations, I stopped at Townsville the first night. Then, having already driven up most of the coast road via Brisbane, I decided to take the inland route south, so headed west towards Charters Towers and then south on Route 55. It is a long and remote road, one favoured by the truck drivers as it is quiet, but the miles clicked over rapidly. I stopped for fuel at Belyando Crossing where we'd had such a lovely early Christmas with an Australian family many months previously, and eventually stopped at Emerald for the night.

I was now on the Gregory Highway, and I continued in the morning but not long after leaving Emerald, I came across a typical Australian sight, a 500-strong herd of cattle being driven along the verge, the Long Paddock, of what was a main road. There were a couple of guys on motorcycles, and a couple on horseback, one of whom was a woman, and there were also some cattle dogs and the whole ensemble was plodding its way, enjoying free fodder from the verge, as it went. As before when we had seen several thousand sheep on the move, these cattle were probably heading for the meatworks.

I continued south, now on the Carnarvon Highway and stopped the next night at Roma. This was a very busy town and all the campsites were full, but the local council had made arrangements for an overflow site at the local racecourse where I joined about 15 other travellers for the night.

The next day, I crossed over into NSW at Mungindi, a rather dismal little place, although I did stop to restock the larder, and on again to Narrabri for the night.

I could have made a last dash to Sydney and arrived late at night, probably totally exhausted, so decided to stop one more night. As ever, I was still keen to try more rural roads when possible and examining the map gave me an idea. There are very few roads leading into Sydney from the north and there looked like an interesting one passing south through the Yengo and Wollemi National Parks.

So from Narrabri, I continued on south, through the delightfully named Coonabarabran, Binnaway and Merriwa, and stopped at Sandy Hollow in the late afternoon ready for a final run into Sydney the next day.

The site at Sandy Hollow wasn't up to much and it was in a narrow valley, so was soon in the shade, and there followed the coldest night in our whole time in Australia. I was glad to have the use of the whole duvet, and wrapped myself up as best I could to keep out the cold – I wasn't used to this. There was frost on the windscreen in the morning and I was keen to get sorted out and on the road as soon as possible.

Finding the road I wanted (Route 69) proved a little difficult as the area around Singleton is a maze of coal mines and newly-built service roads, but eventually I was headed towards Bulga, my target. I was on a narrow two-lane road that twisted and turned through steep gorges and it proved to be a great driving road. Others must have had the same thought as the further I went, the more motorcycles there were, as well as a few sports cars, enjoying the sweeping curves.

Needless to say, Matilda didn't have the handling qualities of these fellow travellers, but we had some fun through the corners and around the various bends until eventually I came to a café that marks, more or less, the halfway point along the 240 km (150 miles) road.

I stopped in the company of plenty of motorcycles and enjoyed a coffee, aware of the huge car park that clearly gets very busy at weekends.

On again through Putty and Colo Heights, still enjoying a great drivers' road, until I finally started entering the outskirts of Sydney and its suburbs.

I was truly back in civilisation. The roads were crowded and hectic. There were traffic lights and a few traffic jams, but in no time at all I was passing through Narrabeen, and then Warringah and up a couple of side roads to our daughter's new home in Freshwater.

It was the end of a beautiful friendship with Matilda and a terrific adventure in Australia. Although initially I had serious doubts about Matilda's ability to take us around Australia on our travels, and was very concerned about her reliability, a very important matter in the Outback, she had been the perfect vehicle for our trip and did us proud. I wished we could have kept Matilda for a future trip but reluctantly we returned her to the Sydney RV Centre and bade her goodbye with a gentle pat on the bonnet and a "Well done, lass."

I had a reunion with Pam and the family, and had a couple of weeks' family time before heading home to the UK.

We had had a ball.

We had seen so much, been to so many wonderful places, and met such lovely, generous and welcoming people.

I'll close by quoting Bill Bryson again. As he said in his book *Down Under*, "There's a lot to find in Australia, but a lot to find it in".

We had tried our best!

Part 9

* Postscript
* Why not have a go?
* Acknowledgements
* Distance chart
* Travel Australia by RV
* A High in the Andes

Postscript

Since coming home, I have heard of some interesting developments on matters reported in the book.

The *Camps 6* directory we used was a valuable reference and is available in various formats. It is updated regularly and the current edition is *Camps 8*.

I have mentioned the Kidman Cattle Empire and as I put the finishing touches to the manuscript for this book, the whole company is being put on the market. The family are in dispute about the company's future and the industry is facing problems due to drought, the high Australian dollar and cattle export bans. The 16 cattle stations remaining in the S. Kidman & Co. empire equate in size to the combined areas of Scotland and Wales.

Sheila Laxon, the British racehorse trainer we met in Karumba, has been found guilty, together with her business partner, of falsifying training records in what was clearly a major case before the Australian Supreme Court (which we had visited). She was found guilty of encouraging an employee to give false evidence, made false entries in horse history records, several other related matters, and her evidence was described by the judge as *"untruthful, inaccurate and unreliable"*. Her credibility has been destroyed and there are substantial costs to be paid.

The young man responsible for the two murders in Quorn on the afternoon we passed through the town has been jailed for 33 years. Both murders were quite horrific as he used an axe to severely mutilate both victims, especially the first, a young lass who, as I mentioned earlier in the book, had spurned his advances.

Like everyone else, Australia is worried about the effects of climate change. The country already has pretty aggressive weather and we encountered extremes of heat on our travels. There was a cyclone and serious flooding in Bundaberg not long after we visited the town, and in several places there were devastating forest or bush fires, including one that led to fatalities.

In the last 100 years, the country has become hotter by almost a full 1C, which doesn't sound much but is a very significant increase. Levels of rainfall have increased in the north of Australia and decreased in the south-east and south-west regions. Increasingly, the rainfall has come as very heavy and intense falls, which increases the risk of flooding. Like everywhere else, sea levels have increased and all these trends in climate change are likely to continue.

The drought in central Australia continues and is particularly severe in south-west Queensland where tens of thousands of stock have had to be slaughtered rather than left to die in their paddocks.

Why not have a go?

If you have read this far, you may be tempted to consider a similar trip yourself. Why not? It needs some planning and my book to accompany this one, *Travel Australia by RV*, will help you on your way. The book covers what I think are all the main points that need considering and will have lots of factual information to help you plan your own adventure.

Blog

My wife and I wrote a blog during our trip around Australia, mainly as a way to keep family and friends up to date with our progress. You are welcome to take a look at: *www.vicandpaminoz.wordpress.com*

Contact

Finally, if you want to ask me some questions about any matter related to travel in Australia, do not hesitate to contact me via:

Email: *vicquayle@aol.com*

Facebook: *www.facebook.com/vicquayle*

Website: *www.vicquayle.com*

Acknowledgements

First, I must thank Pam, my wife, for joining me on this adventurous trip, for tending to my needs, for reading the maps and just – being there. I must also thank her for the help she gave me in writing this book, starting with the diary she kept as we travelled around, in confirming what we did and when, and in checking and proofing the text.

Thanks also to Denise and Mark Barlow, Mandy Newman, Louise Lubke Cuss, Susan Illman, John Fellows, Dave Kitching, and the team at Filament Publishing who all helped in various ways in the production of the book.

I must thank the many friendly and welcoming Australians we met on our travels, too numerous to list but a few must be mentioned - the members of Condobolin Motor Club who made us part of their splendid rally, Leonie and Richard with whom we celebrated Christmas, and Vanessa and Greg whose company we shared for a few days.

My thanks to staff of the Sydney RV Centre who tended to Matilda's needs each time we returned to Sydney and gave us advice and guidance on her workings. They also honoured the buy back agreement we had with them. I would recommend them to any aspiring adventurer thinking of heading to Australia for either a conventional motorhome or caravan holiday, or something more adventurous such as our trip. They have, however, closed their Narrabeen branch and now operate from Penrith to the west of Sydney. Mention me or this book when speaking to them.

The extract from *Down Under* by Bill Bryson, published by Doubleday, has been reproduced by permission of The Random House Group Ltd.

And finally, our daughter, Jenny, and her husband, Daz, who provided us with a base in Sydney from which to recover from our three ventures into the Outback.

Thank you all.

Distance chart

Australia is very big, more or less the size of Europe, and travelling distances tend to be much longer than at home. This chart, which is in kilometres, will help provide some idea of the distances involved in travelling around Australia. The figures can be converted to miles, by dividing by 1.6.

	Adelaide	Alice	Brisbane	Broome	Cairns	Canberra	Darwin	Melbourne	Perth	Sydney
Adelaide		1690	2130	4035	2865	1210	3215	755	2750	1430
Alice	1690		3060	2770	2415	2755	1525	2435	3770	2930
Brisbane	2130	3060		4320	1840	1295	3495	1735	4390	1030
Broome	4035	2770	4320		4125	5100	1965	4780	2415	4885
Cairns	2865	2415	1840	4125		3140	2795	3235	6015	2870
Canberra	1210	2755	1295	5100	3140		4230	655	3815	305
Darwin	3215	1525	3495	1965	2795	4230		3960	4345	4060
Melbourne	755	2435	1735	4780	3235	655	3960		3495	895
Perth	2750	3770	4390	2415	6015	3815	4345	3495		3990
Sydney	1430	2930	1030	4885	2870	305	4060	895	3990	

Travel Australia by RV

How to undertake an extended trip to Australia

By Vic Quayle

Due for publication late 2015

All you need to know about:

- Official stuff (passport, visas, driving licences etc.)

- Finance (income, expenditure, letting your home, banking, credit cards etc.)

- Buying and selling an RV in Australia

- Insurance

- Health and medical issues

- Campsites and free camping

- Flora and fauna

- Nasties (snakes, spiders, jellyfish etc.)

- The Indigenous Peoples

- Coming back home

and more.

Watch out for the publication date on my website at

www.vicquayle.com

Also by the author

A High in the Andes

Foreword by Hannu Mikkola
World Rally Champion

Hardback, 330 pages, colour
photographs, route map and
sample from road book

£25.00 incl. P&P (UK)
Enquire for overseas orders

**Order through
www.vicquayle.com**

Gather together 50 classic rally cars and another 50 4x4s in Rio de Janeiro and send them off on a seven-week rally through the Andes, Atacama Desert, Tierra del Fuego and Patagonia, and you are sure to have a few adventures.

Vic Quayle and his wife, Pam, took their 4×4 over to South America to have the trip of a lifetime. They were not disappointed.

Organised by the Historic Endurance Rally Organisation (HERO), the event was going to be rough and tough from the outset. It would follow in the footsteps of the famous London – Mexico World Cup Rally in 1970 which was won by Hannu Mikkola in a works Ford Escort.

This was a rally of superlatives. One of the longest ever held, it traversed the highest road in the western world; accompanied the world's highest railway line; crossed the world's driest desert, the Atacama; and visited the world's southernmost ever Rally Control on Tierra del Fuego.

And they came home with a Gold Medal for their efforts.

Lightning Source UK Ltd.
Milton Keynes UK
UKOW06f0228180915

258850UK00001B/84/P